PRADO MUSEUM
SPANISH PAINTING

Text: XAVIER COSTA CLAVELL

Photographs, lay-out and reproduction, entirely designed
and created by the Technical Department
of EDITORIAL ESCUDO DE ORO, S.A.

Copyright of this edition for photographs and text:
© EDITORIAL ESCUDO DE ORO, S.A.

The Prado Museum reserves all rights over
the reproduction of its Art Collection.
The photographic reproduction of this edition
has been duly authorized.

22nd Edition

I.S.B.N. 84-378-0288-1

Dep. Legal B. 5687-2003

Editorial Escudo de Oro, S.A.

PROLOGUE

The decision to publish a series of books on different subjects in its interesting collection «Art in Spain», undertaken by Editorial Escudo de Oro, is worthy of the highest praise. This is the first book in the series on the Prado Museum dedicated to that priceless collection of works of art by the greatest masters of painting represented by their most outstanding works, belonging to every school, period and tendency, which both for their quality and quantity contribute to making this Madrid art gallery the best of its kind in the world. This volume is devoted to Spanish painting as, due to the importance of the Prado collection, the Editorial Escudo de Oro has decided to publish two volumes: one (this) on the theme of Spanish painting, and a second on paintings from different foreign schools represented in the Prado.

It would be idle here to dwell upon the works constituting the treasure of the Prado Museum. Throughout the text of the book appropriate references are made to the museum and its most outstanding works. However, it would not be out of place in these introductory lines to point out the extraordinary quality of the illustrations in this volume. The quality of each and every one is an excellent point of reference for the appreciation of the paintings. It is a truly genuine bibliographical panegyric with the high quality illustrations lending exceptional value to the book.

It has not been attempted here to give an exhaustive account of the pictorial content of the Prado Museum, but merely to offer a true image of what this splendid art collection represents within the context of the universal history of painting. This book will be a pleasant and unforgettable souvenir for whoever wishes to browse through its text and its illustrations. The real aim of this book, with regard to the famous Prado Museum, and in the words of the illustrious Marquis of Lozoya is «for it to be, in a far distant hearth, always at hand to converse with you, evoking the sentiments of a few hours spent in the most select atmosphere that could possibly be breathed on Earth».

Angel Oliveras Guart
C. de la Real Academia de Bellas Artes
de San Fernando

The front of the Prado Museum in the lovely wide Madrid avenue of the same name (Paseo del Prado).

THE HISTORY OF THE PRADO MUSEUM

The building which houses this famous collection of paintings, one of the most valuable in the world, was constructed according to plans, now in the Museo Municipal de la Villa, outlined by the architect Juan de Villanueva in 1785, and was originally intended to be the seat of the Natural Science Museum. Built in the shape of a parallelogram, its dimensions are approximately 200 meters in length by 40 meters wide. In Villanueva's time the building was a long rectangular structure of two storeys along the Prado façade and the side overlooking the Botanical Gardens, and of only one storey on the rear and left sides of the building. In 1878 the staircase opening onto the North side was built. The present façade of the Prado consists of a double gallery with an imposing Doric peristyle in the centre. On the Lower gallery are fourteen half pointed arches and four arches with dintels, all of them decorated with busts, niches, urns and statues. The upper gallery is separated from the lower by a cornice and has twenty-eight Ionic columns. A superb portico held up by six large columns, with a small rectangular tower decorated with relief sculpture on top of the lintel, occupies the central portion of the two galleries. On every side of the building are sculptures by Barba, Hermoso and Salvatierra.

A bronze head, one of the most valuable pieces in the Prado Museum sculpture collection.

The original nucleus of the Prado museum included paintings belonging to the Royal collection and consisted of 311 works by Spanish artists, among them paintings by Goya. Later, the collection was enlarged by works from the Flemish and Italian schools reaching a total of 521 paintings in 1821. The collection grew gradually larger during the following years and in 1850 there were over a thousand pictures in the museum. In its initial stages the museum depended exclusively on the Court. Its first curators were the Marquis of Santa Cruz, the Prince of Anglona, the Marquis of Ariza and the Duke of Híjar assisted first by Vicente López and later by the painters Carlos Luis de Ribera and José de Madrazo. The latter was curator of the Royal Museum in 1838 and in 1843 when a new catalogue of its paintings was published. Years later when

The fine sculpture known as the Faun with the Goat.

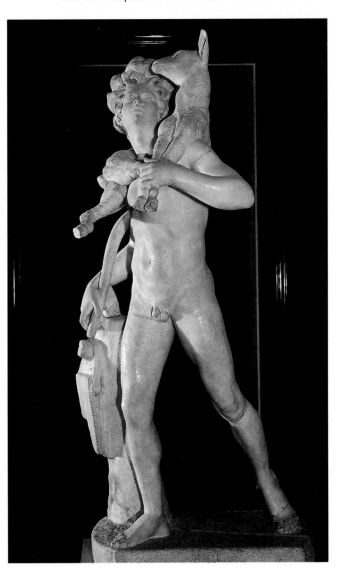

Although the Prado Museum was inaugurated on 19th November 1819 during the reign of Fernando VII –after having been restored due to the considerable amount of damage it had suffered during the Peninsular War–, «the idea of a museum –according to Alfonso Pérez Sánchez– which finally became a reality *for the pleasure and use of the beloved vassals of His Majesty*, as it was expressed in the Gazette of the time, was not a new one», for «since the time of Philip IV, certain parts of the El Escorial palace were already used for the purpose of a museum», and furthermore, «Mengs advised Charles III to create *an art gallery worthy of so great a monarch*, to be conceived in the spirit of enlightenment then prevalent in the whole of Europe during that century».

The idea of the creation of a great Art Museum gained considerable momentum during the reign of Joseph Bonaparte, who toyed with the idea of founding the Joseph Museum. It was, however, the monarch Fernando VII who finally brought about the creation of the museum; he was, it appears, decisively influenced by his second wife María Isabel de Braganza, who died in 1818 without seeing the museum opened.

Sculptures of Diadumenos and Pallas Athena in the Prado Museum.

San Vicente Ribera and Federico Madrazo were curators of the museum construction work was carried out to extend the building. Later, cartoons by Goya drawn for the weaving of tapestries which had been piled up in the palace attics came to enrich the Prado collection. In 1868, when Isabel II was dethroned, the Royal Museum changed its name to the one it bears at the present time–the Prado Museum.

The painter Gisbert became the curator and in 1870 and 1872 the Prado and the Museum of the old convent of La Trinidad were merged by decree; the paintings from the convent were mainly of a religious nature and had almost all come from monasteries and convents affected by the disentailment laws. His decision, though theoretically laudable, gave rise to many practical problems, as the Prado building was not large enough to accommodate two large collections, but the matter was solved by depositing many of the works in different provincial museums.

During this new phase of the Prado Museum, its curators were the painter Sans Cabot, who took office on Gisbert's resignation, and, later, for a second time, Federico de Madrazo, who remained in office from 1881 to 1894. Restoration of the building was undertaken with alterations to the north side including a large staircase, new exhibition rooms and the complete decoration of the whole museum.

Among the new acquisitions in the museum worthy of special mention were the black paintings of Goya, donated by the Belgian aristocrat Emile d'Erlangher, and the magnificent sketches by Rubens which composed the legacy of 200 pictures given to the Prado by the Duchess of Pastrana.

After the death of Madrazo, the painters Vicente Palmaroli, Francisco Pradilla and Luis Alvarez were successive curators of the museum. Around the turn of the century, the Prado Museum received several donations, among which the most outstanding were the Goya pictures entitled *The family of the Duke of Osuna, and Tadea Arias.*

The first XX century curator of the museum was the painter José Villegas, who did important work in the organisation of the museum. In 1912, the Museum Guardianship Com-

Magnificent sculpture representing Emperor Charles I of Spain and V of Germany mastery Fury.

A view of the splendid mural paintings from the Hermitage of La Cruz de Maderuelo, Segovia, a priceless jewel of Spanish Romanesque art and one of the most outstanding treasures housed in the Prado Museum.

mittee was created, its basic aim being to carry out certain alterations in the building and to intensify policy regarding donations and legacies. The building was extended between 1914 and 1920.

Two important events in the history of the Prado Museum stand out during the first quarter of the XX century: the valuable legacy given by Pablo Bosch, and the robbery of some works belonging to the famous Dauphin's treasure. The last event caused Villegas' resignation, and the famous critic Aureliano de Beruete y Moret became curator with the Galician painter Fernando Alvarez de Sotomayor in the post of deputy curator, becoming curator in 1922 on the death of Beruete. The post of deputy curator then fell to the Galician historian Francisco Javier Sánchez Cantón. Under the successful direction of Sotomayor and Sánchez Cantón work was begun to modernise the building and valuable donations such as that of Fernández Durán comprising some 3,000 drawings and almost 100 paintings were received, among them five Goyas worthy of special mention.

Alvarez de Sotomayor resigned in 1931 and the writer Ramón Pérez de Ayala was appointed curator, but as he had also been made ambassador to London, the direc-

tion of the museum was virtually left in the hands of Sánchez Cantón, who carried on in the post of deputy. When the Spanish Civil War broke out, Picasso was appointed curator. but the great painter was never able to take up his post. The contents of the museum, after it was closed down on 30th August 1936, were evacuated first to Valencia and later to Catalonia, being finally deposited in Geneva in the care of the League of Nations until 1939, when they were returned to Madrid.

After this, a new historical phase in the life of the Prado Museum opened up. The painter Alvarez de Sotomayor once again became curator with Sánchez Cantón as his deputy. Improvements were made inside the building using fire-proof materials so as to prevent possible accidents by fire which could destroy the entire collection. During the second term of office of Alvarez de Sotomayor the *Dama de Elche* was given back to Spain as a result of negotiations with the French government. This famous sculpture occupied a room in the Prado from 1942 to 1971, when it was transferred to the collection in the Archaeological Museum of Madrid. Another important factor in the life of the museum was that under Alvarez de Sotomayor's curatorship many considerable donations were received along

The mural paintings in the Prado Museum.

with numerous legacies such as, for example, that of Francisco Cambó, which consisted of valuable works by Botticelli and other painters of the. Italian school. During this phase, the policy of purchasing interesting works was also developed by the Museum Authorities.

On the death in 1960 of Alvarez de Sotomayor, deputy curator Francisco Javier Sánchez Cantón was appointed as his replacement. Eight years later, Cantón was substituted by the historian and scholar Angulo Iñíguez, who held the post until 1970, when the present curator, Professor Javier de Salas, took charge of the museum, with Alfonso Pérez Sánchez as deputy curator.

From this time on, the museum ceased to be an economically independent enterprise, and its administration was taken over by the Ministry for Science and Education. In this administration, the Director-General for the Arts became vice-president of the Guardianship Committee of the Prado. After these changes in administration, the purchases for the museum from 1970 were effected through the Ministry of Science and Education.

THE CONTENTS OF THE PRADO MUSEUM

This museum has one of the most complete collections of paintings in the world. The painting collections are as large, with over 3,000, as they are select, with pictures by the most celebrated of the world's painters. Its collection of sculpture is also important, with more than 400 pieces, as is the collection of valuable objects, especially the so-called Dauphin's Treasure, a set of jewels and diverse objects of exceptional value inherited by Philip V from his father the Grand Dauphin of France which includes priceless pieces of porcelain, cut crystal, gold ornaments, miniatures, ornate dinner services, tapestries, agates, jade, jasper etc.

Paintings from all parts of the world are well represented in the Prado, the following being particularly outstanding: 83 works by Rubens, 40 by Brueghel, 36 by Titian, 14 by Veronese and 6 paintings and 50 drawings by Hieronymus Bosch. As for paintings from the great Spanish tradition, suffice it to mention the existence of 50 works by Velázquez and a similar number by Ribera, 40 by Murillo, 33 by El Greco and no less than 114 paintings and 50 drawings by Goya.

Among the examples of paintings of universal stature are select works from the Spanish, Italian, Flemish, French, German, Dutch and English schools. To visit the Prado Museum is to be initiated into the origins and achievements of the whole of western art.

The original nucleus of the Prado Museum was made up of works by court painters and official portrait painters belonging to the royal courts from the time of Philip II to the reign of Carlos IV, and also of works by Spanish artists up to the end of the XVIII century. As mentioned beforehand, works by painters of the Flemish, and Italian schools were incorporated at a later date.

The overwhelming importance of the Prado collection became evident, however, in the second half of the XIX century, when paintings from the former Museum de la Trinidad were absorbed into its collection. This contribution of religious painting of the Madrid and Toledo schools and of a fine collection of primitives enriched the content of the Prado gallery considerably.

Gradually, after experiencing several vicissitudes –various attempts at arson and robbery towards the end of the XIX century, and also a civil war–, the museum became the splendid show place it is at the present time. In 1946, for example, Romanesque painting was included, having been absent from the Prado hitherto.

During what we might temporarily call the latest stage of the Prado's development, the following works have been incorporated into the collection: Aragonese, Catalan and Valencian primitives, along with works from the baroque

St. Dominic of Silos enthroned as Abbot, *by the Cordovan painter Bartolomé Bermejo.*

tive decorative appeal revealing Byzantine and Oriental influences are a valuable reflection of Spanish Romanesque art. Also of interest are works of Spanish primitive art, particularly the Antependium of San Esteban and the Altarpiece of San Cristóbal.

Gothic art is represented in the Prado by several medieval altarpieces showing the influence of the French and Sienna schools. Particularly outstanding are the altarpieces of Archbishop Sancho de Rolas, by an anonymous artist, and that of La Virgen y San Francisco, from La Bañeza, as well as works by Master Nicolás Francés and the recently-acquired panels by Serra.

«After the second half of the XV century», according to Alfonso Pérez Sánchez, the present deputy curator of the Prado Museum, «the contribution of Flemish realism, inspired by Van Eyck, become a powerful influence due to the Medina fairs and Spain's political leanings towards Burgundy, is felt strongly and insistently in Spanish painting, leading to the emergence of the first Spanish artists of universal projection. The impeccable objectivity of Jan van Eyck or the master of Flemalle took on, in several Spanish artists, a pathetic note which is almost expressionistic and in their vigour and roughness and the oriental profusion of gold, they are unmistakably the fruit of our

The Martyrdom of St. Catherine, *by the primitive Castilian painter Fernando Gallego.*

schools of Cordoba, Granada, Seville and Valencia, which have either been bought or generously donated and have thus contributed to the broadening of the historical and artistic perspective of this famous Madrid art gallery.

The oldest paintings in the Prado are the Romanesque frescoes from the Hermitage of San Baudilio de Berlanga (Soria); and from the apse of the Hermitage of Santa Cruz de Maderuelo (Segovia); these paintings with their primi-

Reredos of the life of the Virgin and of St. Francis *by Nicolás Francés.*

best primitive artists». Outstanding among these Spanish artists represented in the Prado are the Castilian Fernando Gallego, the Corbodan artist, established in Aragon, Bartolomé Bermejo –with his work *St. Dominic of Silos Enthroned as an Abbot*–, Pedro Berruguete –who introduced Renaissance styles into Castile– and several anonymous artists.

As for works from the XVI century, the following are of note: *Saint Catherine*, by Hernando Yáñez de Almedina –in whose art Pérez Sánchez observes «a strong echo of the art of Leonardo da Vinci, mixed with a Venetian richness of colour»–; *The Virgin of the Souls* by the Toledo-Granada Mannerist Pedro Machuca; *The passing of the Virgin* by Correa de Vivar, *The Relief of Genoa by the Second Marquis of Santa Cruz* by Antonio Pereda and *The Adoration of the Magi* by Friar Juan Bautista Mayno. (Other important painters such as Juan de Juanes, Morales, Sánchez Coello and El Greco are dealt with in separate chapters).

The most famous works of art in Spanish history can be admired in the Prado, some examples being: *The Gentleman with his hand at his chest, Christ bearing the Cross, The Baptism of Christ, Pentecost or The Resurrection*, by El Greco; *St. Buenaventura receiving his habit from St. Francis*, by Herrera the Elder; *The Labours of Hercules or St. Isabel of Portugal,* by Zurbarán; *The Surrender of Breda, Las Meninas, Prince Balthasar Carlos, «The Cousin», «The Simpleton from Coria», Aesop, The*

Spinners, The Drunkards and *Don Gaspar de Guzmán, Count-Duke of Olivares* by Velázquez; *The Children with the Shell*, *The «Soult» Immaculate Conception* and *The Patrician's Dream*, by Murillo; *The Miracle of the Well*, by Alonso Cano; *Jesus debating with the Doctors* by Valdés Leal; *The Infanta Isabel Clara Eugenia by Sánchez Coello; The Virgin and Child worshipped by St. Louis, King of France*, by Claudio Coello; *The Naked Maja, The Robed Maja, The Maja and the Hooded Men, The Crockery Seller, The Mason Wounded, The Family of Charles IV, The Charge of the Mamelukes, The Executions of the 3rd of May, The Colossus, Saturn devouring one of his children, The Witches Sabbath* and *A Dog* by Goya. This is but a brief list of some of the most outstanding Spanish paintings to be seen.

All the fine pictures, besides the sculpture, the Dauphin's treasure, and other valuable pieces in the Prado are distributed throughout a hundred spacious rooms on the ground, first and top floors of the building, and also in the basement. As there is such a vast quantity of exhibits which tends to increase constantly, it has been necessary to adapt some corridors and staircases to exhibit still more paintings and pieces of sculpture.

Not long ago the Prado Museum merged with the former Museum of Modern Art whose contents were essentially works by XIX and XX century artists; the latter has now become an independent section of the Prado with a separate deputy curator and enjoying a certain degree of autonomy. The annex which was once the Modern Art Museum is in the Casón del Buen Retiro and the works of XIX century artists owned by the Prado now adorn its walls –among these the most noteworthy are works by the portrait painter Vicente López, who painted a popular picture in which Goya appears.

Since 1819 the Prado Museum has been publishing catalogues with an inventory of its contents; the first of these being edited by Luis Eusebi, the janitor of El Prado.

Although the Royal Museum, the origin of what is now the Prado Museum, was inaugurated in 1819, «it was really the monarchs of the House of Austria», according to Alfonso Pérez Sánchez, «who instigated the collection we can now see in the Museum. Though we know of the interest in art of Queen Isabel the Catholic, and of the works she commissioned in Granada and Madrid to decorate her palaces which have been preserved, none of these have reached the Prado. We have to wait till the reign of Charles I of Spain, the great Emperor of Europe, to find pictures and ornaments belonging to him. A patron of Titian, who painted his portrait on several occasions, he also acquired works by Correggio, Miguel Coxien, Antonio Moro, and was connected with works by Memling and Jacobo Bassano now in the Museum».

Charles I's son Philip II was also deeply interested in painting. A patron of Titian as his father was, he commissioned several important works, among them the painting entitled *Philip II*, now in the Prado. He also patronised Morales and set up a fine gallery. Because of the admiration Philip felt for the original and disconcerting art of Hieronymus Bosch (clearly an early precursor of the Surrealists) the Prado is fortunate in possessing an extremely representative collection of the paintings of this Flemish genius. This royal collection of the so-called «prudent King» was one of the most valuable of its time.

Although many of these paintings were destroyed when the Prado Palace was burnt in 1604, quite a few of them can still be seen in the Museum. Philip III increased the collection with works by Pantoja and Carducho. However, it was the Duke of Lerma who contributed most to the enriching of the royal art gallery by his acquisition of several paintings by the great Flemish master Rubens, now one of the major attractions of the Prado Museum. But it was Philip IV who most contributed to the future splendour of this Madrid museum. This monarch not only appointed Velázquez as his court painter during his reign –which made the painter of *Las Meninas*, along. with Goya, the best and most widely represented Spanish artist in the Prado–, but he also patronised the acquisition of paintings from the Italian school and several pictures by Rubens. Philip IV

The transfer of the body of James the Elder I and II: The Embarkation at Jaffa *and* The Removal to Galicia, *two panels from the same altarpiece, attributed to the Ximénez Circle (second half of the XV century).*

 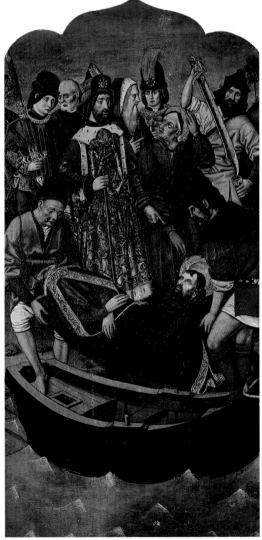

The Knight of Montesa Virgin, *by Paolo de San Leocadio, reflecting the artistic vigour and expressive charm of Spanish art in the XVI century.*

converted his palaces of El Escorial, La Zarzuela, and the Casa de Campo into genuine museums. His short-lived successor, Charles II, whose court painter was Carreño, also increased the Royal collection then amounting to some 5,339 paintings distributed throughout the various palaces. The first of the Spanish Bourbons, Philip V, followed in the tradition of the preceding monarchs and his second wife Isabel of Farnese, an ardent admirer of Murillo, acquired several paintings by this artist from Seville and others by painters of the Flemish and Dutch schools. A great fire broke out in December 1734, devastating the Alcazar Real in Madrid and destroying no less than 530 priceless paintings, thus seriously depleting the contents of the future Prado Museum. The Prado owes its large collection of Goyas to Charles III and Charles IV, and this constitutes one of the most prestigious sections of the museum.

The Adoration of the Magi and The Nativity, *two works which belong together, attributed to Rodrigo de Osona –Osona the Elder– (documented in Valencia from 1464 until, probably, 1484) and his son, Francisco de Osona –Osona the Younger–. Religious themes predominate between the mid-XIV century and the second quarter of the XVI, a period considered by many scholars to be the first golden age of Spanish painting. There was a flowering of religious painting in Spain towards the middle of the XV century, dense and vibrant and often of unknown authorship, marked principally by Italian and Flemish influences. Works from this period of Spanish painting are characterised by their ingenuous quality and the delightful charm of their expression.*

The Archangel Michael, *by an unknown Spanish-Flemish artist in around 1475.*

St. Catherine, a panel attributed to Yáñez de la Almedina (first half of the XVI century).

15

The Last Supper, *one of the most characteristic works of the Valencian artist Juan de Juanes.*

JUAN DE JUANES

This painter from Valencia, whose real name was Vicente Juan Magip, was born around 1523 and died in 1579; the son of Vicente Magip who was also a painter, Juan de Juanes was greatly influenced by Raphael and the Mannerists and was even called «the second Raphael». There is some confusion between the paintings done by the father and those done by the son, and in many cases it is unclear which painting was done by whom.

It would appear that Juan de Juanes learnt his profession in the studio of Paolo de San Locadio and that it was in Italy where he was so impressed by the masters of the Italian school, especially Raphael and Sebastiano de Piombo. «Juan de Juanes –writes Valeriano Bozal in his History of Art in Spain– is a precursor; his painting was to become the model for ecclesiastical art for several years and after an interruption during the first half of the XVII century, this influence was to appear again in the paintings of Murillo and other religious artists».

This painter is, in effect, the perfect example of the pious Christian trying to reflect the religious spirit of Catholicism in his art. He was an excellent draughtsman with a fine sense of plasticity when combining colours, his art being closely related to the Mannerist aesthetic. His rich use of colour is –according to Alfonso Pérez Sánchez– «com-

parable with the most famous Flemish Romanists. It is evident that while Magip, the father's, painting directly evoked the Italian school, Juanes must have specially admired the masters from the Low Countries, and thus he stylised and purified his technique in emulation of them».

Juan de Juanes is one of the most popular of the masters of Valencian painting. His pupils, among them one Fray Nicolás Borras and the blessed Nicolás Factor, all painted in a pious vein with a Mannerist style.

Even a much later painter, Francisco Ribalta –born in Solsona in 1564 and died in Valencia in 1628– copied *The Last Supper*, one of Juan de Juanes' most representative works, now in the Prado.

All the work of this painter is sweetly sentimental with figures in peaceful attitudes and faces reflecting spiritual calm. There exists a remote influence of Leonardo in his work but generally it is a mere Mannerist imitation. Everything is too beatific and of a stereotyped loveliness expressed in a too conventional language. With all his qualities, Juan de Juanes is not able to reach modern sensibility even though he often tried to abandon his beatific style of art with scenes, for example, from the *Martyrdom of St. Stephen*, a painting from the main altar in the Valencian parish church of the same name which was bought by Charles IV in 1801 and is now in the Prado.

JUAN PANTOJA DE LA CRUZ

Juan Pantoja de la Cruz was born in 1553 and died in 1608. He was court painter during the last years of the reign of Philip II and the first years of that of Philip III. When the court moved to Valladolid, Pantoja lived there from 1602 to 1606.

This painter followed Alonso Sánchez Coello's footsteps in the difficult art of court portrait painting, both being inestimable historians in paint of their respective contemporary experiences.

Although Pantoja is well represented in the Prado with his magnificent portraits of Philip III and the Queen Doña Marguerita, his most famous work is perhaps the portrait of Philip II as an old man which now hangs in the library at El Escorial. There are also some interesting works of his in the Convent of Las Descalzas Reales in Madrid, in particular the portrait of *Isabel Clara Eugenia*.

In the painting of this artist there can be seen a certain break with Mannerism, along with the appearance in the portraits of the first stylistic incursions of the baroque. Pantoja did many religious paintings within the Mannerist aesthetic, but with a use of colour evidencing a desire for liberty of the imagination. In this sense, his work *St. Nicholas of Tolentino,* now in the Prado, is particularly interesting.

Philip III *and* Queen Margarita*, portraits by Pantoja de la Cruz which form a pair.*

Fragment from The Triumph of Bacchus*, a painting from Ribera's early period, inspired by Caravaggio.*

RIBERA

It is known for certain that José de Ribera was born in Játiva (Valencia), but the exact date has remained obscure. According to some authors, he was born on 12th January 1588, others say it was 12th January 1591 and yet others allege that the artist came into the world on 17th February 1591. Ribera was of humble origin –his father worked, some say, as a shoemaker, others affirm he was a soldier– but it seems that, although his family wanted him to study letters, he began to work in Ribalta's studio from an early age.

Ribera lived for some time in Italy where he was known by the nickname of «lo Spagnoletto» (The little Spaniard). He also lived in Parma, Rome, and Naples, where he was married in 1617. During the early days of his stay in Italy, Ribera was beset with difficulties, leading an irregular

bohemian life until he married Catalina Azzolino, the daughter of a painter, when his life began to take on a more ordered tone.

Ribera's arrival in Naples coincided with the height of the power of the Society of Jesus, who were in charge of several monastic orders and at their centres of learning patronised painting which was in agreement with their socio-religious principles for the decoration of churches. It was the time of the beginning of the Counter-Reformation and its influence was clearly reflected in art forms which were pathetic in concept with baroque tendencies. Ribera became easily integrated into this developing tendency, which emphasised the mystical expression characteristic of the Counter-Reformation compared with the more rational and balanced human aesthetic of the Reformation. Ribera enjoyed the advantage of being an excellent draughtsman besides a

Jacob's Dream *is one of José de Ribera's most famous works. This is a painting of clear Venetian influence in which the recumbent human figure, placidly dreaming, contrasts with the dark tones of the painting, characteristic of Ribera's second creative period.*

The Martyrdom of Saint Philip *is perhaps the best-known work of «El Españoleto». In it the gloom pervading his second creative period is most evident. Ribera was born in Játiva and formed in Italy, where he lived for many years, a creative period when his paintings are immersed in a markedly gloomy atmosphere of stark realism.*

St. Paul the Hermit, *a work showing Ribera's unique and personal artistic temperament.*

The oil St. Jerome *is one of Ribera's most exultantly realistic works. In this painting, «El Españoleto» achieves a truly splendid artistic study of human anatomy, a realistic facet contrasting harmoniously with the aura of spirituality which illuminates the expression on the saint's face.*

born colourist. Both these qualities contributed to establishing his artistic prestige in an eminently Counter Reformation Naples which at that time was also a Spanish Viceroyalty.

There are three distinguishable stages in the work of Ribera. The first, between 1616 and 1624, is marked by an evident Venetian influence, inundated with light, but –in the words of Alina Cuoco–, «in spite of his inspiration based on the works of Caravaggio, Ribera reveals himself above all in a spirit of academic classicism which is grotesque and completely subjective or, as others would have it, completely Spanish». There is, of course, in this artistic phase of Ribera's a certain humorous vein, very characteristic of the Spanish subjectiveness already mentioned and which can also be appreciated, taking into account the difference in time, in the painting of Goya or Picasso.

The second discernible stage in the art of Ribera is from 1624 to 1638. This is the so-called dark period of «lo Spagnoletto». The picture entitled *St. Andrew* –which can be seen in the Prado Museum– belongs to this phase and is a fine example of this facet of Ribera's development.

Finally, in the third stage, Ribera s painting became more transparent and on occasion can be related to the luminous elegance of the art of Velázquez.

Among the 50 canvases by Ribera in the Prado, the following are perhaps outstanding as being represen- tative of the different periods of the painter's development: *The Martyrdom of St. Philip*, showing the dark tones characteristic of the second phase, with some colour and light counter balancing slightly the oppressively gloomy atmosphere hovering like an almost threatening presence in the painting; *St. Jerome*, an impressively realistic picture where the artist demonstrates his ability in this fine study of the anatomy of the human body, which contrasts effectively with the spiritual expression on the face of the Saint; and *Jacob's Dream*, a picture in which the presence of the Venetian influence in the colours contrasts with the form of the picture where in spite of its dark element the figure of Jacob is evocatively human, peacefully immersed in a dreamless sleep.

This work, entitled Saint Andrew, *is another example of the tenebrism which characterised Ribera's second period.*

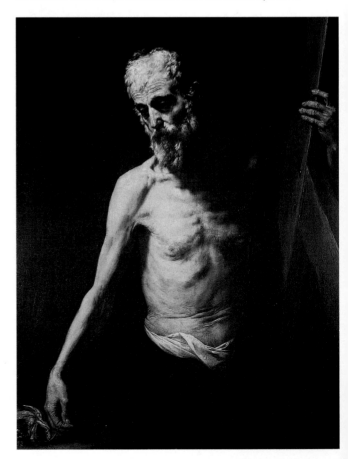

The Virgin and Child, *by Luis de Morales.*

LUIS DE MORALES

Born in Badajoz around the year 1520, this painter died C. 1586 in the same city, although he lived in Seville, where he painted, amongst other pictures, *The Virgin with the Bird*, in Portugal, where he made the altarpieces for Santo Domingo de Evora, and in Italy. Nevertheless, the greater part of his work was done in the province of Extremadura, whose churches still possess the best altarpieces by Morales, at, for example, Giguera la Real, San Martin de Plasencia and Arroyo de la Luz. In Seville he was the pupil of the Flemish artist Pedro de Compana from whom he learnt his refined technique. Students of Luis de Morales' painting have said that he represented, in a way, an «evocation of the mediaeval» in composition and that his style was basically rooted in Gothic. It has also been said that his art was influenced by Leonardo and that in his expressionism there were certain Germanic elements. Valeriano Bozal states that Morales, «on the one hand looks towards the classicism of Leonardo and to the Mannerism of Raphael and his pupils, to Central European Mannerism and even to the Flemish passion for detail, while on the other he gives a foretaste of the dark character of the Andalusian painters and those of Extremadura with the sentimentalism of the baroque decadence expressed by Murillo and his followers». Among Morales' works in the Prado, his *Virgin and Child* is noteworthy, executed with an impressive perfection of Mannerist technique, it has a delicate spiritual quality.

PEDRO BERRUGUETE

The exact date of his birth is unknown; but he was born in Paredes de Nava, a village in the province of Palencia. Pedro Berruguete lived in Italy for several years where he decorated the palace of the Duke of Urbino. Around the year 1483 he did some work for Toledo Cathedral and later painted several altarpieces in his native village, and in different places in the province of Burgos and also in Avila. Berruguete died in 1504 and his name was perpetuated in the history of art through his son Alfonso, a sculptor of some importance and also a painter.

In Pedro Berruguete's work both the Italian and Flemish influences are assimilated. Regarding the latter, Valeriano Bozal asserts that sometimes the Flemish influence is «so great that we seem to be in the presence of a work by a pupil of Van der Weyden, as for example in the diptych representing *The Crucifixion and Piety* in the cathedral at

The Virgin and Child, a fine work by Berruguete, who was born in Palencia.

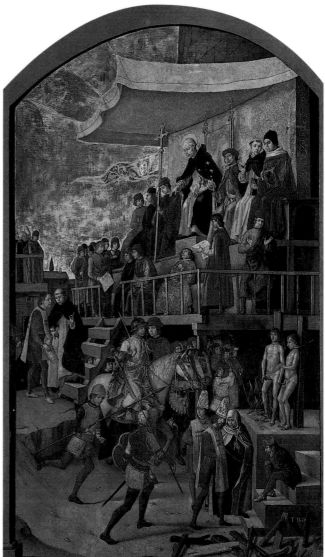

Auto de Fe presided over by Saint Dominic of Guzmán, *an oil painting by Pedro Berruguete.*

Palencia. However, Paul Guinard observes in Berruguete a simple deep sentiment whose «primitive» character is accentuated by the frequent recourse to backgrounds in goffered gold. The altarpieces of St. Thomas de Avila with his miracles (lives of St. Thomas Aquinas, St. Dominic and St. Peter the Martyr), his scenes of prayer or sermonising are redolent of a monastic chronicle or even of a documentary work (like the *Auto da Fe* in which St. Dominic pardons the condemned men)».

Among Berruguete's works in the Prado, the most outstanding are the aforementioned *Auto da Fe and Virgin and Child,* a sober painting with great subtlety of expression.

This painting by El Greco, representing The Saviour, *is an illustrative example of the original creative personality the famous Cretan painter acquired after settling in Toledo.*

EL GRECO

In spite of being born in 1541 in Candia (Crete) and being first a citizen of Venice, Domenico Theotocopuli is universally and justifiably considered to be a genius of Spanish painting. Italians and Spaniards called him Dominico Greco, or simply El Greco, the Greek, as little is known of the painter's early years on his native island. Apparently, the family of Domenico Theotocopuli enjoyed considerable wealth which enabled him to have an excellent education. According to Philippe Daudy, El Greco «was a soli-

tary character, independent, melancholy and proud; he experienced at the same time the desire for sumptuous pleasures and spiritual profundity».

About the year 1567, El Greco was, according to information, already in Venice, where his brother Manusso lived and who helped him during the initial period of his stay. Before going there, it is said that El Greco was connected with a school of painting in Crete run by Theophanes of Crete. Valeriano Bozal offers the hypothesis that «he underwent the influence of iconography which was never to abandon him, especially as regards the construction of space typical of these works and their expression. At that time and possibly until 1566, his works were signed *Domenicoa* and were inspired by prints and engravings with Italian and Byzantine elements already in evidence».

El Greco's stay in Venice was for him a true artistic revelation. He worked in Titian's studio and some art historians say that the court painter of Charles I and Philip II referred to Domenico in a letter to Philip II mentioning a certain «Greek of great worth, a pupil of mine». The teaching of Titian greatly influenced El Greco and to a large extent conditioned his future aesthetic, outlining the personal style which was to make him immortal.

In Rome, where he went around 1570, El Greco became acquainted with Julio Clovio, a painter of miniatures who was well connected with the Roman Curia and the protégé of Cardinal Grimani. Clovio recommended him to Cardinal Alexander Farnese, who allowed him to live in his palace.

As a result of his stay in Rome, where he remained sev-eral years, the work of Domenico Theotocopuli was influenced to some extent by Roman Mannerism. It was in the Eternal City where his artistic prestige began to be acknowledged after being influenced by Titian, Tintoretto, Michelangelo and Bassano during the years of his stay.

Before setting out for Spain, El Greco went once again to Venice. Ana Pallucchini is of the opinion that «he must have stayed there till 1576, leaving Venice in that year, perhaps to escape from the plague which caused the death of Titian, afterwards to go to Spain».

It appears that he went first to Madrid, where he probably got to know Doña Jeronima de las Cuevas, an aristocratic lady who some say was his mistress and others his lawful wife, by whom he had a son called Jorge Manuel who might be the young gentleman painted by El Greco in the portrait in the Museum of Fine Arts in Seville.

It is known that in 1577 El Greco was present in the city of Toledo, where he obtained a definitive artistic forma-

Christ embracing the Cross, *by El Greco.*

St. Sebastian, *a painting from El Greco's final period.*

25

St. Andrew and St. Francis, *an oil by El Greco showing clearly the Cretan painter's tendency to lengthen figures.*

St. John the Baptist and St. Francis of Assisi, *by El Greco from the early-XVII century.*

Indubitably one of El Greco's most famed paintings is The Gentleman with his hand at his chest, type and symbol of the Spanish gentleman of the period. In this work, the great painter excels himself, reaching the highest place in universal art.

tion to make him one of the greatest painters of all time.

El Greco certainly owed a great deal to Toledo; it would be practically impossible to appreciate the real meaning of his work if one were to omit or underrate the influence that the marked personality of that city had on the spirit of the great painter. Toledo contributed enormously to the consolidation of the highly personal aesthetic of El Greco. There is, nevertheless, a danger in accepting facile arguments based on predestination or providence easily established *a posteriori* but with little or no value when it is a question of the real truth. It must be established that El Greco was in no way predestined to go to Toledo nor was he impelled to go to this city by any supernatural force as has been insinuated by some authors with a too vivid imagination. It is much more con-

vincing to accept the facts as they really are. El Greco did not hear any magic voice calling him nor did he intuit that only in Toledo could he find his true self and reach the climax of his great art. He came to Spain and went to Toledo for strictly rational motives, as he went to find work in El Escorial which was under construction at that time, or had been taken there by whichever of his patrons was concerned with him then, such as, for example, Don Pedro Chacon or Don Luis de Castilla. Anyhow, El Greco's presence in Spain and in Toledo can easily be explained. What is most probable is that he came to work there to consolidate his formation as an artist and at the same time to improve his standard of living. All this is certainly much less attractive and poetic than the series of gratuitous fictions which usually arise to explain the presence of El Greco in Toledo and his later undeniable

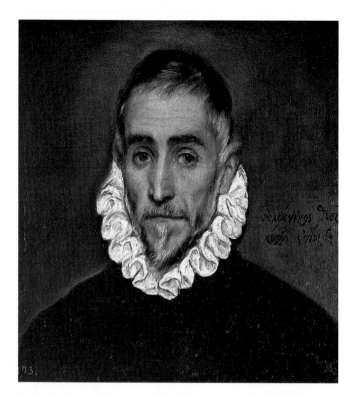

Portrait of a gentleman, *a characteristic work by El Greco.*

The Virgin Mary, *an oil by El Greco.*

and positive identification with the lovely city on the Tagus.

It would appear that El Greco lived if not in opulence at least in some comfort from his arrival in Toledo up to the time of his death. After working on the altarpiece in the Convent of Santo Domingo, he began to enjoy great prestige as a painter in the city of Toledo. This enabled him to rent a fine house overlooking the Tagus and to live by painting, at the same time immersing himself in the spirit of that original and complex imperial city, assuming from the fresh springs of Toledo the feeling and vocation of an Empire mixed with the prophetic mysticism of the Spain of that time.

Apparently, about the year 1580, he painted the picture entitled *Martyrdom of St. Maurice and the Theban Legion*. In 1586 he began to paint one of his most successful and

The Doctor (Dr. Rodrigo de la Fuente?), *by El Greco. The identification of this famous Toledo doctor is based on a portrait of him in the National Library.*

grandiose works: *The Burial of Count Orgaz*. He was commissioned to do the work by the Church of Santo Tomé, where this admirable painting is still to be found, undoubtedly one of the jewels of world art.

His *Dream of Philip* was apparently painted about the year 1579. *The Crucifixion* belongs to 1600. The following year he *painted St. Bernard of Sienna, St. Paul* and other important works. The impressive *View and Map of Toledo* was probably painted in 1609.

El Greco worked incessantly until his death. Commissions came in abundance. He carried out some architectural work commissioned by the Augustine convent in Madrid in about 1590, and worked for the Illescas Charity Hospital during 1603, and in 1604 began to work on altarpieces for the Church of the Virgen del Rosario in Talavera de la Reina. El Greco scarcely left Toledo during the last years of his life and died in his adopted city on 31st March 1614. El Greco's death caused great sorrow in Toledo, which had welcomed and adopted him, and with which the painter had identified himself with such affection.

The swan song of Domenico Theotocopuli, which was painted in the last year of his life, was a work *entitled The Assumption of the Virgin*.

Góngora, the great Spanish poet vindicated by the Generation of '27, wrote a splendid sonnet as an epitaph for the tomb of the painter:

Esta en forma elegante, oh peregrino,
de pórfido luciente dura llave
el pincel niega al mundo más suave,
que dio espíritu al leño, vida al lino.

Su nombre, aún de mayor aliento dino
que en los clarines de la Fama cabe,
el campo ilustra de este mármol grave:
venérale, y prosigue tu camino.

Yace el Griego. Heredó Naturaleza
arte, y el Arte estudio, Iris colores,
Febo luces, si no sombras Morfeo.

Tanta urna, a pesar de su dureza,
lágrimas beba y cuantos suda olores
corteza funeral de árbol sabeo.

These verses by Góngora, with their diamond-hard precision, harmonise with the grave seriousness of El Greco and his works.

Later on, another great Spanish poet, Rafael Alberti, succeeded in capturing the original message of Domenico Theotocopuli, as shown by these fine lucid verses:

The Holy Family, *by El Greco.*

Aquí, el barro ascendiendo a vértice de llama
a luz hecha salmuera,
la lava del espíritu candente.
Aquí
la tiza delirante de los cielos
polvoreados de cortadas nubes,
sobre las que se vuelcan
en remolinos o de las que penden,
agarrados de un pie, del pico de un cabello,
o del cañón de un ala,
ángeles de narices alcuzas y ojos bizcos,
trastornados de azufre,
prendidos por un fósforo traído en un zigzag del aire.
Una gloria con trenos de ictericia,
un biliar canto derramado...

Pentecost, *a painting in which El Greco's original treatment of space can be appreciated.*

In this painting by El Greco, The Crucifixion, *Christ's expression is more one of grave reflection than of pain.*

When trying to situate El Greco in his period, two factors must be taken into account regarding Spain, his country of adoption, which determined his ethical and artistic attitudes.

Firstly, Spain at that time was the supreme military and political power in Europe, which meant it was to all intents and purposes the most powerful country in the civilised world.

The Baptism of Christ, which originally formed part of the altarpiece in the College of Nuestra Señora de la Encarnación de los Agustinos Descalzos, Madrid, and now in the Prado Museum, consisting of two planes whose figures are lengthened according to El Greco's aesthetic canons. The finely-toned colour is splendidly applied, with flashes of light the Cretan painter was the first to achieve.

Secondly, it must be realised that there was an underlying factor that affected and was closely related with the political, the social and the religious, which was the omnipresent arm of the Holy Inquisition; at the time of El Greco's arrival in Spain, this institution had the greatest power in the land.

Therefore, these two factors in association were substantially reflected in El Greco's work dating from his arrival in Toledo. Despite his highly personalised aesthetic, El Greco created during his time in Toledo works of sublime majesty and he did this, either consciously or intuitively, inspired by the fact that the country in which

In The Annunciation, *El Greco gives free rein to his artistic fantasy.*

The figure of Jesus Christ emerges naked from the Earth and ascends towards heaven in this oil by El Greco entitled The Resurrection, *whose composition is in accordance with the master's singular aesthetic.*

he lived and with whose spirit he had become identified–Spain–was at the zenith of its power. His original style contributed to the accentuation of the imperial tenor of his paintings.

Aesthetically, El Greco's work can be considered to be in advance of his time, anticipating by several centuries the most daring and successful experiments of modern art. All his work is, in this sense, a long-term premonition in art.

«For XX century artists,–writes Julio E. Payró–, who are not mystics but who, in the forms adopted by art, appear to find a basic rehabilitation of spiritual values, together

The Trinity, a painting from El Greco's early period, with marked Italian influence.

The Adoration of the Shepherds, *a painting by El Greco showing all his virtuosity in composition, colour and execution. In his work, this great painter expounds the basic principles of his original aesthetic concept, a veritable vanguard canon centuries ahead of developments in universal painting in general.*

The Coronation of the Virgin, *by El Greco, in which the Virgin is surrounded by the founders of the religious orders, an angel, and cherubins.*

painters in the Prado. Of the 33 works by him in the Madrid collection, the following are perhaps the most outstanding:–*The Gentleman with his hand at his chest*– one of his most famous works and a portrait of extraordinary quality, sober in composition, execution and colouring, from which there emanates that spiritually-condensed humanity which no one has painted better than El Greco and which, in spite of the profane nature of the subject, there is, in the seriousness of the face and in the attitude of the gentleman with his hand at his chest, an impressive religious feeling; *The Crucifixion* is an immense canvas 312 by 169 cms. of Christ on the cross. His figure is in the centre of the painting, is measurably distorted and in an attitude not of pain but rather of grave reflection, at His feet are four figures, one at the right of Jesus with a gesture of suffering, and the remaining three showing serene devotion, giving the impression of being imbued with the divine presence: *The Baptism of Christ*, an oil painting with all the characteristics of El Greco's later period, the elongated distorted forms typical of the

Saint John the Evangelist *is one of El Greco's most attractive paintings.*

with a marked aversion to materialism, El Greco is without any doubt the most «modern» of all the painters belonging to the Renaissance-Baroque cycle and, therefore, the one to whom they feel most attached because of their many affinities. To be quite frank, it is our century that has resuscitated El Greco, about whom almost nothing was ever said, that is if he were ever spoken of at all before 1902, when a retrospective exhibition of his work was organised for the first time in the Prado Museum in Madrid».

El Greco is without any doubt, for his period, the painter most in the forefront as regards aesthetics and who reflects in his paintings of the Toledo period the spirit of an imperial Spain, arch-defender of the Catholic dogma. He is therefore a special case within the context of pre-Goya Spanish painting. In Velázquez –the precursor of Impressionism– if one digs deep through his subtleties, there exists a critical sense. In El Greco there is no critical sense, only fervour and exaltation. Later on with the arrival of Goya who burst in upon the scene of Spanish and universal painting, everything would be overturned-styles, and ideas. Goya has exaltation, a critical sense and a renewed style. He is an open rebel. Velázquez rebelled internally and El Greco only aesthetically.

Domenico Theotocopuli is one of the best represented

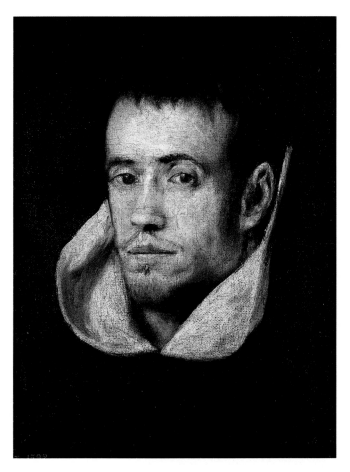

A magnificent portrait of a Trinity, or Dominican monk, *showing all El Greco's artistic skill.*

The Holy Shroud. *The spirituality emanating from this head is one of the most characteristic features of the faces painted by El Greco.*

painter's aesthetic norm with a splendid use of colour subtly applied, not lacking in those details which up to that time only El Greco had been able to succeed in creating, at least with the intensity with which they expand in all directions throughout all his pictures; *St. John the Evangelist* is one of El Greco's most evocative paintings, from the simple composition there emanates a natural quality, and the use of colour, within the intentionally sober tone, is harmoniously adapted to the symbolic nature of the subject. The predominant figure is St. John, the head being a prodigious example of virtuosity in which the painter has poured all the richness of his most refined spirituality.

Other works of special interest are those entitled *The Adoration of the Shepherds,* in which, as Valeriano Bozal says, «the contrasts of light reach unsuspected heights and the union and coherence of the two worlds (earth –where the shepherds worship the Child; and Heaven– with the choir of angels) is complete with no separation or interruption nor any duality in composition»; *The Annunciation*, a painting whose composition –according to Eugenio D'Ors– «proceeds from the first phase of Italian influence, and the forms that fly mingle there with passing forms, some of them correct architecturally, with Heaven and earth juxtaposed»; *Portrait of a Doctor (Dr. De Lafuente)*, a work which D'Ors found close to that of Tintoretto; *The Trinity,* which reminded the author of *Three hours in the Prado Museum* of «the works of Michelangelo in his old age», a painting in which «even here the body of Christ seems wonderfully athletic» and «still in the world of flying forms, he reminds the world that all is transient...». All El Greco's work in the Prado Museum captivates and induces reflection. He is a thrilling phenomenon of plastic creation. Fray Hortensio Paravicino correctly says of the painter in a particularly apt verse:

Crete gave him life; Toledo, his paint brushes.

A portrait of Francisco Pacheco, *the Sevillian painter. Velázquez was his pupil and married one of his daughters.*

VELÁZQUEZ

Diego Rodríguez de Silva y Velázquez, without any doubt one of the eminences of universal art of all time was born in the luminous city of Seville on 8th June 1599. To be born in such a lovely city would in a way be an ideal beginning for a painter, for in Seville, light, sky and air constitute such a dazzling and beautiful presence in themselves that it would indeed be incomprehensible that the sensibility of a born artist like Velázquez could remain indifferent to its special charms.

It must have been in that same city where, one day, in the words of Rafael Alberti, in his beautiful poem dedicated to the painter of *Las Meninas*:

Life appeared one morning
and begged him
-Paint me, paint my portrait
as I really am or as you
would really like me to be.
Look at me, here, I am a passive model,
still, waiting for you to capture me.
I am a mirror searching for another mirror...

Velázquez was the son of Juan Rodríguez de Silva, a Portuguese noble from Oporto, and Jerónima Velázquez, who descended from an aristocratic Sevillian family. Young Diego, who later took his maternal surname, began studying philosophy and Latin rhetoric, but soon realised

Las Meninas *is one of the most harmonious and finely-balanced paintings in universal art, and the most perfect example of light and shade and its harmonious use in painting.*

Velázquez's portrait of Queen Mariana of Austria *is a work of remarkably simple execution, free of all rhetoric concession.*

stern character and young Velázquez was not able to put up with his irascible teacher. He had to leave his studio and then began as a pupil in the studio of Francisco Pacheco.

Velázquez fell in love with Juana, one of his teacher's daughters, and married her in 1618 when he was no more than 19 years old. During the first year of his marriage he painted Juana Pacheco's portrait which now hangs in the Prado Museum.

Four years later, Velázquez went to Madrid. During his stay in the capital he painted a portrait of the poet *Don Luis de Góngora y Argote, a copy* which can be seen in the Prado. Apparently things did not go too well for Velázquez during his first stay in the capital, and he was obliged to return to Seville and establish himself once more in his native city.

However, the following year, 1623, the painter returned to Madrid and succeeded in getting into the service of the

Velázquez was probably assisted by one of his pupils in this fine portrait of The Infanta Margarita of Austria.

that neither syllogisms nor the study of Latin had anything at all in common with his incipient artistic vocation.

Apparently his father did not take long to discover his son's true vocation. Far from being opposed to his son's inclinations, Don Juan Rodríguez de Silva decided to help him to educate his artistic feeling and so put him in contact with Francisco Herrera the Elder, in whose studio Velázquez began his apprenticeship.

It appears that Herrera the Elder, though a man of evident talent and a painter of some note, was possessed of a

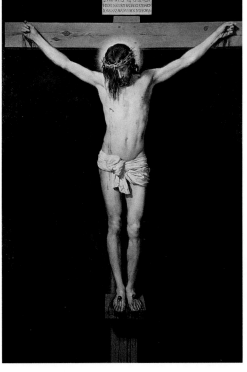

The Adoration of the Magi, *by Velázquez in 1619. All the figures represented are portraits, of the king at an advanced age with Francisco Pacheco, the young king with Velázquez and the Virgin with his wife, Juana Pacheco.*

Velázquez painted this Coronation of the Virgin *in around 1641-1642 for the Oratory of the Queen's room in the palace in Madrid.*

The famous Christ Crucified *which inspired Miguel de Unamuno to write one of his most beautiful paintings, and which Velázquez painted for the Convent of Las Monjas de San Plácido. The figure of the crucified Christ is perfectly drawn and enveloped in a finely-toned range of light. Velázquez makes this painting a masterpiece of artistic restraint approaching, whilst always retaining his unmistakable personality, Greco-Latin classicism.*

In this canvas, Mercury and Argos, *Velázquez recreates a mythological theme, once more demonstrating his prodigious gifts as a painter and his fine perception of colour and composition. There is something magical in the atmosphere of the painting, especially in the two human figures, which contrasts with the impressionistic realism of the sea in movement.*

A view of the Villa Medici garden in Rome, *painted by Velázquez during his stay in the Eternal City.*

Pablo de Valladolid, *court jester, in a portrait by Velázquez from around 1633.*

King, His Majesty Philip IV as a gentleman of the bedchamber. On October 6th 1623 he became the monarch's court painter with a salary of 20 *escudos* a month. This promotion from gentleman of the bedchamber to court painter was obtained as a reward given by the King himself after having admired the equestrian portrait Velázquez did of him. During this same year, 1624, Velázquez also painted the Portrait of the Count-Duke of Olivares, made a *Bust of the King* (both of these are now in the Prado),

In this painting, entitled Cardinal Infante Don Ferdinand of Austria, *Velázquez creates one of his most admirable scenic symphonies.*

The magnificent portrait of Prince Baltasar Don Carlos *shows the young prince surrounded by a masterfully-rendered landscape with the most varied shades and tones, difficult in the extreme to capture. The composition is perfect, revealing Velázquez's excellent taste, a hallmark of all his oils and one of the principal characteristics of his unsurpassed art.*

Menippus and Aesop. *Velázquez's sensitivity vibrates in these magnificent oils, as it does in all the masterpieces of the Golden Age painters in their portrayals of picaresque Spanish types.*

These portraits of buffoon –The Child of Vallecas, Francisco Lezcano, The Buffoon Sebastián de Morra, The Buffoon Calabacillas and The Buffoon Diego de Acedo, «The Cousin»– along with those of monarchs and the powerful of the time, provide artistic information –of the highest quality– which are not only indispensable for understanding the society which surrounded Velázquez, but also to discover the fundamental details of Velázquez's life.

Portraits of Philip IV as a young man, Philip IV *and* The Infante Don Carlos*, three paintings showing Velázquez's enormous talent for the portrait, an artistic facet in which he reaches great heights in universal painting and gives a true picture of the society in which he lived.*

painted a *Portrait of a Man*– now in the Munich art gallery– and *Calabacillas de la Revolera,* now in the Donaldson collection in London.

Between 1625 and 1627, he painted several pictures, among them the Portrait of *the Infante Don Carlos, Philip IV and Portrait of Juana Pacheco*, all three now in the Prado.

In 1628, Velázquez made the acquaintance of the great Flemish painter Rubens, who had come to Madrid on a diplomatic mission. Rubens and Velázquez admired each other as painters and became excellent friends. It would not be over-daring to imagine that Rubens, a more mature painter at that time and older than Velázquez, should influence the Sevillian artist not only by his advice but also by the example of his masterly pictorial works. Certain critics have pointed out the Fleming's influence in the painting entitled *The Triumph of Bacchus*–popularly known as *The Topers*–, in which there is certainly a substantial similarity in apotheosis of sensuality which emanates from the best of Rubens' works in the Prado.

On 10th August 1629, Velázquez embarked in Barcelona for Genoa accompanied by Spinola. This stay in Italy was for him a sort of aesthetic revelation. His creative horizons became broadened after studying the works of the great masters of Italian painting, especially those of Michelangelo and Raphael. Velázquez stayed in Italy until 1631, visiting Venice, Ferrara, and Rome, where he remained for a year. In the Eternal City, he depicted the marvellous Roman gardens in two fine studies which are now in the Prado Museum. From Rome he went to Naples and on returning to Madrid, devoted himself exclusively to painting superb portraits of Philip IV and his courtiers until 1636.

In 1637, Velázquez painted several pictures of great artistic value apart from his court themes. These are: *The Buffoon Calabacillas*, erroneously known as *The Simpleton from Coria, The Child of Vallecas, The Cousin and Portrait of the Sculptor Martínez Montañés*, all four now in the Prado Museum.

From 1638 to 1648 the following works, among others, were painted by Velázquez (all of then in the Prado gallery):

Coronation of the Virgin and *Portrait of Count Benavente*. Velázquez retained the creative spirit and the prodigious technical mastery which characterise the whole of his vast work until the last years of his life. In 1655, he painted *The Spinners*, in 1667; *Las Meninas* –a masterpiece–, and about 1658, *St. Anthony* and *St. Paul, first hermit*, all three of which are now in the Prado.

On 7th April 1660 Velázquez was sent by the King to the Isla de los Faisanes in the post of Equerry when the Infanta Doña María Teresa was sent to France, having been betrothed to Louis XIV on the signing of the Treaty of the Pyrenees; however, the painter became ill and had to return to Madrid, where he died on August 6th 1660.

His was a life of intense activity, blessed with the great gift of artistic creation and upheld at all times by a genuinely transcendental vision of humanity. The physical death of Velázquez causes us to think of him, like Alberti, reading his verses dedicated to the painter:

Queen Margarita of Austria, wife of Philip III, *in another portrait by Velázquez.*

Equestrian portrait of Philip IV. *In the background is a symphonic blend of colours with the subtle predominance of a silvery grey in the sky, appearing to symbolise the end of an ill-fated reign.*

Queen Isabel of France, wife of Philip IV, *a portrait Velázquez completed in 1635-1636.*

These two oils, Prince Baltasar Carlos *and* Gaspar de Guzmán, Count-Duke of Olivares, *are two of Velázquez's finest portraits. The first was done in 1635 or 1636. This is a graceful painting executed with perfect technical mastery. In the second, painted in around 1634, Velázquez makes every effort to favour his model as far as may be. Nonetheless, he reproduces the unpleasant expression on the Count-Duke's face with unrelenting faithfulness.*

The Spinners, *or* The Fable of Arachne, *an oil by Velázquez. The quality of the draughtsmanship and colouring of this canvas rival the technical mastery Velázquez displays in his famous work* Las Meninas.

More life, yes, more life,
and your painting,
O Painter, having lived,
more than real painting would have been
painting suggested,
a slight trace, the dilution of a created form.

Velázquez has been called «the painter of truth». «Painter of truth», yes, certainly but what truth? It is not, of course, the well-known common truth which is evident and timidly concrete, but quite the opposite, it is a dynamic individualised truth. His own truth; Velázquez's own truth.

So much has been said of Velázquez being a supremely realistic painter that he has even occasionally been accused of being a mere copier –albeit a masterly one– of strictly objective reality. But Velázquez is something more, much more: he is a genuine re-creator. A re-creator of genius. He sees what is essential and isolates what has been imprinted on his painter's retina. Velázquez gives emotional animation to the life which surrounds him and also criticism, criticism as weighty as it is severe. His artistic clairvoyance penetrates the outer trappings and apprehends the subtlest vibrations in the soul of beings or things. Velázquez's pictures are never historical inventories of merely physical things. The painter of *The Spinners* transports real atmospheres onto the canvas, that is true, but always with a dominating spirituality. There is a central motive in his works which acts like a protagonist, though

Velázquez, as a realist painter, makes a faultless study of the naked body in this work, entitled Vulcan's Forge. *Painted in 1630, he piece was acquired four years later by Philip IV.*

sometimes only in appearance, alive, shot through with vibrant emotions or inimitable personal traits –often the key to evident pathological abnormalities rather than to a vigorous personality– and a host of ancillary motives, diluted, dominated by the central theme, although certainly not always. Perhaps it would not be too daring to say that Velázquez is the great precursor of Impressionism. On the attribution of this quality to the author of *The Surrender of Breda*, Maurice Seralluz states the following: «Often eliminating the surrounding form, Velázquez in our view, in certain parts of his paintings carried out a vibrant *tachisme* with mixed or juxtaposed touches; in this way he modelled either a landscape or the human body, material, jewels and diverse objects. More binding accents translate

luminous reflections and sparkling vibrations, half tints more fluid and transparent are used with effect».

Velázquez's painting is in no way aseptic; it is a world of life or the life of a world. And for this reason one can develop this life in oneself once one is immersed in the magic of the work of Velázquez, so full of surprises in interpretation as is the impressionism of which he was en early forebear.

After Goya, Velázquez is, with Ribera, the best represented painter in the Prado, each of them with 60 canvases hung there. All the most famous of Velázquez works are in the Prado, beginning with *Las Meninas,* considered by critics in general as his masterpiece.

It is an enormous canvas, 318 cms. by 276 cms. original-

The Topers –the real title of this painting is The Triumph of Bacchus– is one of Velázquez's most popular works. The painting emanates a powerful dionysiac force.

ly entitled *The Family of Philip IV*. The painter's own studio is reflected in the painting and the artist appears in a corner of the canvas as if painting the portrait. The sensation of life produced in the spectator by the painting could not be more genuine. The studio is in semi-darkness, lit by a shaft of light which shows up the graceful figure and blonde hair of the Infanta Margarita and brings out the dress and jewels she is wearing. Everything in the picture is delightfully spontaneous. Velázquez has masterfully succeeded in capturing the transient nature of the moment, cleverly juxtaposing light and shade. The painter's palette shows a fantastic richness of colour. But what astonishes even more is the extraordinary variety of shades of grey revealing Velázquez's insuperable technique. This work belongs to the mature age of this highly gifted painter.

Another masterpiece is *The Spinners*, whose real title is *The Fable of Arachne*. This is an interior scene where what surprises us is the marvellous contrast of colour and the difficult but perfectly achieved quality of the movements of the figures forming part of this extraordinary composition. The atmosphere of this interior appears to be prodigiously illuminated. This is a picture which undoubtedly influenced the XIX century impressionists.

Also of great importance in the context of Velázquez's work is the painting known as *The Surrender of Breda* –popularly called *The Lances*– in which the act of surrender of Nassau and his men is faithfully reflected. The picture is, in human terms, a true lesson in good taste, quite apart from its strictly technical aspects, all of them solved extraordinarily well; this good taste is one of the characteristics of Velázquez's painting, and not only of his painting but of him as a person. Spinola, one of the main figures in the picture, welcomes Nassau with courtesy when he hands over the keys of the city. Velázquez underlines this chivalrous gesture of Spinola's, but doesn't forget to emphasise the joyful pride felt after victory in battle. Where is this joyous pride to be found in the painting? It is symbolised by the martially erect lances of the conquerors.

The following paintings by Velázquez are justly famous: *The Triumph of Bacchus –or The Topers–*, a magnificent painting with a dionysiac strength emanating from it; *Vulcan's Forge –*which reveals the influence the painter underwent during his first stay in Italy–; *Equestrian Portrait of Philip IV; Don Gaspar de Guzmán, Count-Duke of Olivares; The Prince Baltazar Carlos; «The Cousin»; Aesop; «The Simpleton from Coria»* and *Our Lord Crucified,* which inspired a fine heart-felt poem by Unamuno.

The Lances, the popular title given to Velázquez's The Surrender of Breda, *is a master class in artistic conception, composition, colouring and execution. The famed painting shows the surrender of Nassau and his men in what is, in human terms, a lesson in good taste. Spinola, one of the principal figures in the picture, on the side of the victors, welcomes Nassau courteously as he hands him the keys to the city. The artist highlights Spinola's chivalrous gesture, but does not omit the joyful pride of the victor of any battle, symbolised by the martially erect lances of the conquerors.*

St. Luke *as a painter (a self-portrait of Zurbarán?) before Christ on the cross, one of Zurbarán's finest works.*

ZURBARÁN

Francisco de Zurbarán was born in Fuentes de Cantos (Badajoz) around 1598 and died in Madrid in 1664. One of the great figures of Spanish painting, he was the son of rich peasants, but little is known of his childhood. Actually, it can scarcely be said that there exists any biography of Zurbarán in the sense of a conventional biography full of information, facts and anecdotes. His real biography is in his artistic production and his work in general.

Bernardino de Pantorba cites several legends, though these are mostly uncorroborated, in which Zurbarán is the hero; among them is the following: «an anecdote picked up by Don Juan José Serrano states that in his village, Zurbarán did a caricature of a certain rich landowner named Silverio de Luarca with such spitefulness that the man ridiculed decided to take revenge, which he did by

killing the artist's father. Having committed the crime, the murderer fled, taking refuge in the court. The legend, adding more colour to the event, goes on to tell how the son of the murdered man, after some time had passed, saw and recognised the odious Silverio in Madrid one night and ran him through with his sword, thus avenging the blood of an innocent man».

«Zurbarán's painting», says Valeriano Bozal, «does not illuminate, it transfigures, and does not proceed from any more or less real or natural source, than from the figures themselves, from the very bodies of nuns and saints».

Of the works of Zurbarán in the Prado, the following must be mentioned: *Vision of St. Peter Nolascus*, an allegorical painting in the purest style of Zurbarán; *Apparition of St. Peter the Apostle to St. Peter Nolascus, a work of* fantastic naturalistic colour; and a magnificent *Still Life*, perfectly executed with the austere grace characteristic of Zurbarán.

Vision of St. Peter Nolasco, one of Zurbarán's best-known allegorical paintings. This large work –179 x 223 cms.–, was commissioned by the Order of the Merced de la Calzada, who wished a painting of an episode from the life of their founder saint. The composition, execution and colouring are in the purest Zurbarán style, that is, with the characteristic mystic aura the artist gave his works.

In this canvas, Zurbarán impresses us by depicting the half-naked body of Saint Peter nailed to an inverted cross. The composition and colouring of the painting, entitled The Apparition of St. Peter the Apostle to St. Peter Nolasco, are quite fantastic, while the execution is completely naturalistic, demonstrating once more that separation between idea and execution which is a constant in Zurbarán's work.

Of these two works by Zurbarán, one entitled, The Defence of Cadiz against the English, is on a warlike theme and not in the painter's usual style. The other, a Still Life, is, however, a fine artistic achievement. Here, measured good taste is in evidence, difficult to describe adequately. Zurbarán's characteristic austere grace is paramount in this picture, though he was often the servant and not the master of this quality. The still life is formed by four pots, made of copper, bronze or earthenware, placed simply on a table. The work shows Zurbarán to be an unquestioned master of the still life study.

*Christ dead, held by an angel, a painting by Alonso Cano, versatile artist
from Granada who was also an outstanding sculptor and architect.*

ALONSO CANO

Born in Granada in 1601, Alonso Cano died in the same city in 1667. Besides being a painter, he was also a renowned sculptor and architect. There are three basic stages in his life: one which took place in Seville until 1638, during which time he devoted himself to various architectural projects and to sculpting several altarpieces; the second stage, which took place in Madrid, where he was commissioned by the Count-Duke of Olivares in 1638 to paint several important works, among them the altarpiece at Getafe: and, finally, the third stage, beginning in 1652 and culminating in his ordination as a priest.

Alonso Cano almost always lived a turbulent life, and characteristic of this was the drama caused by the murder of his second wife. The painter was arrested and, although absolved of all blame, left Madrid, taking refuge for a time in the Carthusian monastery of Portaceli near Valencia. Later he settled in Granada where on more than one occasion he had brushes with the Cathedral authorities.

In Seville, Alonso Cano was a fellow pupil of Velázquez in Pacheco's studio. He married in 1626 and on becoming a

The Miracle of the Well, *a painting by Alonso Cano executed with the utmost technical perfection.*

The Virgin and Child, Two Kings of Spain *and* A King of Spain, *three paintings amply demonstrating Alonso Cano's pictorial skills.* The Virgin and Child *is an evocative lyrical poem executed with delicate mastery, whilst that of the last two surprise us with their vivid colouring.*

widower soon afterwards, he married for a second time, his wife being the daughter of the Sevillian painter Juan de Uceda.

Lafuente Ferrari considers Alonso Cano «the point of balance between Zurbarán and Murillo, between the serene objective naturalness of Velázquez and the baroque exaltation of the painters of the past generation».

The best works of Alonso Cano are impregnated with a delicate religious lyricism. A subtle aura of melancholy seems to softly caress his dead figures of Christ and his saints.

The following paintings of Alonso Cano are now in the Prado Museum: *The Miracle of the Well*, a magnificent painting reminiscent of the best technique of Velázquez; an excellent *Self-portrait*; *The Virgin and Child*, in a technique similar to Murillo's; *A King of Spain; and Two Kings of Spain*. Altogether excellent samples of the smooth loveliness characteristic of the art of this painter.

The infantas Isabel Clara Eugenia and Catalina Micaela, *by Alonso Sánchez Coello in around 1571.*

ALONSO SÁNCHEZ COELLO

Considered for along time as a painter of Portuguese origin, Sánchez Coello was actually born in 1531 in the locality of Benifayó not far from Valencia, and died in 1588. From an early age he lived in Lisbon with his grandfather, who had taken part in campaigns waged by the Portuguese in Morocco.

Sánchez Coello obtained a pension from King John III of Portugal and studied in Flounders between 1550 and 1554 with the portrait painter Antonio Moro, who influenced him notably in his training as a painter.

From 1555 he worked in Castile in the service of Philip II, who appointed him court painter. Sánchez Coello painted many portraits of the King and other members of the Spanish court during this time. He also executed numerous works of a religious nature and decorated, along with other painters, the altars in the church of El Escorial.

Sánchez Coello is a painter of importance in quantity as well as quality whose works are dispersed throughout European and American museums. His most valuable paintings are in the Prado and in the Museum of Las Descalzas Reales in Madrid. Others of his works can be seen in Buckingham Palace in London and the Rudnice Palace in Czechoslovakia.

Sánchez Coello was without doubt one of the most characterised painters of the Spanish court. «Just as El Greco created another world by transfiguring this one», according to Valeriano Bozal, Sánchez Coello creates another world, the world of the court, the King, of which this world is only a reflection».

Sánchez Coello was influenced by Moro and also by Titian. However, according to Paul Guinard, his painting «is very Spanish in its greatness and in its monotony... All his portraits are similar in their severity in the manner of dress, –black with a gold chain in the portraits of the men, enriched with pearls and several necklaces in those of the women– and in their attitude; they are tapered figures, leaning on a piece of furniture, dangling a glove or a fan with a certain air of haughtiness and melancholy».

Among Sánchez Coello's work in the Prado Museum the following are worthy of special mention: *The portrait of the Infanta Isabel Clara Eugenia*, a lovely child of thirteen who looks at us from the canvas with eyes suffused with that melancholy poetry that characterises the passing from childhood to adolescence, and whose clothes, richly embroidered, and her laces and jewels, are meticulously painted in a masterfully acquired Flemish technique; *The Infanta Catalina Micaela of Austria, Duchess of Savoy* and *«Prince Carlos»*, both portraits in which Sánchez Coello emphasised his mastery of technique.

Three magnificent oils, Prince Don Carlos, The Infanta Isabel Clara Eugenia *and* Catalina Micaela of Austria, Duchess of Savoy, *showing the extraordinary gifts of Sánchez Coello as a portrait painter. Alonso Sánchez Coello was Philip II's court painter, and is represented in the Prado Museum by an invaluable collection of works.*

The Triumph of St. Augustine, *a fine example of Claudio Coello's pictorial style.*

CLAUDIO COELLO

This artist was born in Madrid in 1642 and died there in 1692. The son of a bronzist of Portuguese origin and a Castilian mother, Claudio Coello was a pupil of Francisco Rizi and lived in Rome for four years from 1656 to 1660. He began by painting pictures on religious themes for churches in Madrid and by doing frescoes on both religious and secular subjects. He was appointed the King's painter in 1683 and three years later he decorated the palace, but the pictures were destroyed during the fire of 1734.

Claudio Coello was considered by his contemporaries to be the most important painter of his generation. He can also be said to be the last painter of importance in the Spanish Golden Age. He was a portrait painter of considerable merit and perhaps represents, as Alfonso Pérez Sánchez suggests, the apotheosis of monumental and decorative baroque. An able fresco artist together with Mitelli and Colonna from Bologna, he was also the master of the large altar painting, thus making «in a highly personal way, a dynamic composition, open and decorative with strict realism in the details, especially the faces, and in the accessories of still life, all being in consonance with the painting of the first half of the century». Some outstanding works of Claudio Coello's in the Prado are: *The Virgin and Child surrounded by virtues and saints*, of Flemish influence, and *The Triumph of St. Augustine.*

The Virgin and Child surrounded by the Virtues and Saints *is one of the best works representing the Madrilenian artist Claudio Coello in the Prado Museum. Claudio Coello's religious painting was considered by his contemporaries as the finest during the period from the late-XVII century to the early-XVIII, a period when the baroque style dominated Spanish art.*

This canvas, entitled The Virgin and Child worshipped by St. Louis, King of France*, in a marked baroque style, is characteristic of Claudio Coello's art.*

Magnificent Self-portrait *by Bartolomé Esteban Murillo, an exact copy of that now in the National Gallery, and one of the popular Sevillian artist's finest paintings.*

MURILLO

Bartolomé Esteban Murillo was born in Seville on 31st December 1617, although some authors state that he was born on 1st January 1618, and died on 3rd April 1682 after falling from scaffolding in Cadiz while painting the upper parts of the picture entitled *The Mystic Marriage of St. Catherine of Alexandria.*

The painter was from a large family in poor circumstances who lost his father while still young. Murillo's difficult childhood could have caused him to reflect a less kindly image

of life in his paintings than one normally finds. But although sweetness seems to be the general tone in his art, there are exceptions to this on occasion. In general, Murillo is not attracted by anything unpleasant and tends to reject any brusque encounter with crude reality, but sometimes there is a vague allusion to the poverty which he probably experienced at first-hand in his childhood. Obvious examples of this acquaintance with poverty –lived with greater or less intensity but contemplated from close quarters– appear in several pictures of Murillo's on profane subjects such as *The Young Beggar, Boys eat-*

ing Grapes, Boys playing dice or even *The Little Fruit Seller.*

Murillo was attracted by painting from a very early age and had his first lessons in the studio of Juan del Castillo, where Alonso Cano also worked, and after 1639 he began to live off his earnings as an artist. He always lived a very simple life, constantly and decidedly devoted to painting. In this respect, it can be said that Murillo lived a happy life. He was a man with a peaceful disposition who limited himself strictly to the world of painting. It is impossible to discern a critical sense of surrounding reality in his work. He is a conformist painter, voluntarily integrated in the soci-ety in which he found himself. Altogether, Murillo painted some 400 pictures in 40 years, and some of these, about 100, are of very large dimensions. He spent practically his whole life painting. The fact that he was so devoted to this and that in spite of his hard childhood Murillo was never a resentful person doubtless contributes to a favourable impression of him as a person and subjectively justifies the kind, rather glorifying view of human life reflected in his work. It does not matter greatly whether this view corresponds exactly to the truth, as neither this reality nor its background are artificial inventions of Murillo's but facets of the work showing the painter's real feeling.

The Immaculate Conception, *known as the «Soult Virgin» as it once belonged to the French marshall of that name, who appropriated the painting during the Peninsular War.*

The Conception of Aranjuez, *a work whose colouring is typical of Murillo's painting, with the rich blend of colours used to form the background atmosphere.*

It is impossible to understand either Murillo or his painting correctly without appreciating these facts: his complete identification with Seville and all that the city of the Giralda represented in the XVII century. The light, perfume, grace and passionate religiosity of Seville are all present in Murillo's works. It is necessary to have witnessed the Holy Week processions in Seville to be able to understand the whole meaning of the Murillo-Seville association.

This lovely and enchanting city on the Guadalquivir, with its Torre del Oro, Cathedral, Giralda, Alcazar and Santa Cruz neighbourhood –where, incidentally the painter is buried– is part of Murillo. Seville and its spirit constituted the artistic placenta for the formation of the sentiment and aesthetic of the artist who painted *The Children with the Shell*. The city was able to understand this and Murillo is, and was in his lifetime, the most popular artist in Seville.

The Immaculate Conception of El Escorial, *an evocative painting of one of the themes closest to Murillo's heart.*

Apparition of the Virgin to St. Bernard, *which Murillo painted in around 1660.*

Although he began to live from his painting around the year 1639, he was not able to excel as an artist until 1645 when the Franciscans commissioned him to paint several pictures for their convent, among them *St. Thomas of Villanueva giving alms to the poor, The Angels' Kitchen* and *St. Diego of Alcalá giving food to the poor.*

In 1648, the painter married Doña Beatriz Cabrera, a lady from an aristocratic family. Murillo was established as an artist and had begun to be the master of his own style, abandoning the influence of Velázquez, Ribera and Zurbarán which had been evident in his first pictures. Thus a new artistic phase began for the Sevillian painter, commencing with the *Immaculate Conception with a monk writing on the mystery* for the cloister of the Augustine monastery in Seville, and *The Vision of St. Anthony,* a canvas commissioned for the baptismal chapel of the University of Seville.

The painter enjoyed great prestige in his native city and

Immaculate Conception, *another beautiful interpretation of the theme, of which Murillo once more demonstrates his complete mastery.*

This painting, of St. John the Baptist as a Child, *is another fine production. The work is perfectly composed, outstanding particularly in the highlighted red of the cloth which partially covers John the Baptist.*

Somewhat similar to the previous painting, The Good Shepherd *has a more profane air. Here, too, is the figure of the child beside a lamb, and the same innocence illuminates the faces of both children, but there is no mystic sentiment in* The Good Shepherd, *and the tenderness is fundamentally human.*

Murillo's painting, popularly known as The Children with the Shell *but whose official title is* Jesus and St. John the Baptist as children, *is perhaps the Sevillian painter's most attractive work.*

his name was known and admired outside Seville. Nevertheless, he continued to live in a simple manner, happy in his work. In 1660, he opened an academy in La Lonja in Seville. His life went on in the same pleasant way without any violent happenings or monetary difficulties. Murillo and his wife had no less than nine children, three girls and six boys, but most of them died at an early age with only three surviving: Gabriel who apparently emigrated to America around 1680, then Francisco and Gaspar, who became monks.

Murillo was a friend of the painter Valdés Leal, although they broke off later; and it appears that on a certain occasion, when looking at his friend's picture entitled *Death surrounded by its attributes*, he exclaimed, «Friend, this picture can only be looked at with one's hand over one's nose».

He was also an intimate friend of Don Miguel de Manara, the founder of the Charity Hospital whose body rests in the church crypt before the altar. Murillo painted several large pictures for this church, among them *St. Isabel of Hungary*, still kept in the Charity Hospital. Don Miguel de Manara, Murillo's friend, is said to be the person by whom Zorrilla the poet was inspired to write his drama *Don Juan Tenorio*.

Saint Anne and the Virgin, *another work demonstrating Murillo's technical mastery.*

After 1645, Murillo began to find himself as an artist completing the process of humanisation already begun in the second phase of his artistic development. However, he had to wait a few years for his style to acquire that quality which lent a poetic light to his best pictures. «One must wait for the first and one of his loveliest and largest *Virgins*, the one painted in 1652, now in the Seville Museum», says Philippe Daudy, «to see this warm style of Murillo's in all its splendour. It was with this canvas that his reputation was firmly established. His *St. Leandro and St. Isidoro*, painted in 1655, are two great paintings in the broad baroque manner.

The final and most famous style of Murillo –the «vaporous» style– began with *The Vision of St. Anthony*. After that, the influence of Venice predominated definitively over the Flemish influence in the painter's work. In a cloudy sky, full of the angels which were the hallmark of the painter's fame and which later on provoked so much aversion, we have the typical Murillo composition. The angels do have the virtue of animating the backgrounds of pictures with a mysterious movement and make a striking contrast with the face of the Virgin, the figure of Christ or the Saints; this type of portrait reveals the essence of Murillo's talent». There are some 40 paintings by Murillo in the Prado

Murillo painted The Adoration of the Shepherds *between 1650 and 1660. This is a classical religious scene in which the Virgin shows the shepherds the naked Child. Murillo avoids clichés through superb composition and a colouring rich in range and tone.*

In The Holy Family with little bird, *which he painted in around 1650, Murillo produced one of his most cheerful and unusual works within the religious themes which predominate his oeuvre. The scene is simple and homely, nothing reveals to us at first sight that we are contemplating personages anointed by divinity.*

The Virgin of the Rosary, *a painting by Murillo which emanates serene simplicity, its figures tenderly made human.*

Rebecca and Elisher, *a painting Murillo completed between 1660 and 1670, is one of the masterpieces of his mature years. The canvas was acquired by Isabel of Farnese, a great admirer of Murillo, virtually his discoverer in the XVIII century, in Seville in 1729. It was kept in the Royal Palace of La Granja until 1746.*

Murillo's version of The Dissipation of the Prodigal Son *serves as a counterpoint to another work he produced on this Biblical theme, entitled* The Prodigal Son feeding the swine.

The Patrician's Dream, The Virgin and Child *and this* Landscape *show Murillo's prodigious creativity and mastery of technique. The colouring in these three paintings, quite different one from another, contrasts with the tones characteristic of most of Murillo's work, in which his preference for softer tones is revealed.*

In this unusual Landscape, *Murillo appears to depart from his own aesthetic and in some way to intuit the still distant Romantic movement.*

Museum, the most outstanding being, *Jesus and St. John the Baptist as children*, better known by the popular title of *The Children with the Shell*, where the painter reflects this traditional ideal so intrinsic in him. It is one of his most characteristic works. The ineffable sweetness of the children reaches heights of the most delicate and expressive poetry in paint. The subject couldn't be simpler, one of the children is giving the other a drink out of a shell while a lamb and three angels contemplate the innocent scene. The composition of the painting is admirable and the light and blending of colours delicately done. The flesh tones of the children are simply enchanting and there is a lightness of touch apparent in the whole painting which produces a masterly evocation of an idyllic atmosphere.

Another work of great interest is the «Soult» *Immaculate Conception,* probably painted around 1678, in which Murillo reveals all his artistic maturity. His proverbial sweetness is, in this work devoted to the evocation of feminine spontaneity revealed in the Virgin's whole attitude. The face is one of great beauty and the religious sentiment transfiguring the features does not detract in any way from its human appeal. The figure of the *Immaculate Conception* –divine, but also a woman– is surrounded by angels and enveloped in that vaporous atmosphere characteristic of Murillo's later phase. This canvas was painted for the Hospital for the venerable priests of Seville and was appropriated by Marshall Soult during the Peninsular War. Soult's descendants sold the picture by public auction in May

1852 when it was bought by the French government. For almost a century it hung in the Louvre Museum, but was returned to Spain in 1940 after an exchange of works of art organised by the French and Spanish governments; since that date it has been in the Prado.

Other excellent works by Murillo are *The Holy Family with a little bird*, a curiously joyful painting with a simple and familiar theme which at first sight does not reveal the fact that we are contemplating divine persons; *The Virgin of the Rosary,* a serenely simple painting, evocative and endearingly human with a splendid use of colour and soft tones in exquisite shades finely drawn and spontaneous in composition. *The Adoration of the Shepherds*, rather a contrived subject, but excellent in composition, with a rich use of colour and exquisite human expressions on the faces of the shepherds worshipping Jesus, also a lovely face of the Virgin; *Christ on the Cross* –there are two paintings in the Prado on the same subject–, painted by Murillo towards the end of his life, and this is one of his most dramatic works; *Ecce Homo, Rebecca and Elisher, The Prodigal Son, abandoned, The Gentleman of Golilla* and an excellent *Self-portrait.*

Nicolás Omazur, Galician lady with the coin and Old Woman spinning *are three works by Murillo showing the Sevillian artist's enormous gifts as a portrait painter.*

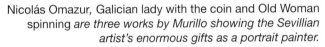

The Duke of Pastrana is one of the most outstanding works of Juan Carreño de Miranda, whose paintings reflected the atmosphere of the court of Charles II.

CARREÑO

Juan Carreño de Miranda was born in Avilés in 1614 and died in 1685. Descended from an Asturian family of the petty aristocracy, he first studied painting in Valladolid and then in Madrid. Carreño was a man with distinguished manners, refined and not only fond of painting but also of letters. He reached Madrid when he was still very young and was lucky enough to make the acquaintance of Velázquez and become his friend, and Velázquez protected him at the beginning of his career and introduced him at court.

Carreño de Miranda became known as a painter of religious subjects and in 1669, on his own merits, was appointed painter to His Majesty, obtaining the post of court painter two years later.

«Carreño —says Paul Guinard— is a witness to the reign of Charles II as eloquent as was Velázquez in the reign of Philip IV. His atmosphere is that of the court, sumptuous and sad, in which the influence of pomp and etiquette in the style of Versailles is apparent, but all is in a minor key, bathed in a sort of greyish twilight. Carreño is an unforgettable painter; first, among the pale mirrors and con-

Portrait of Peter Ivanowitz
Potemkin, Russian ambassador,
*one of Carreño's most personal
works.*

This portrait of the sickly Charles II *shows Carreño's mastery of the pictorial art.*

His painting is based on the use of crepuscular lights. He seems to be announcing in some of his best pictorial achievements the painful transition not from one reign to another but from one dynasty to another, from the House of Austria to that of Bourbon.

«Carreño –as Guinard observes– is less of a court painter strictly speaking than Velázquez. In his work, the Spanish aristocracy occupies an important place; slim, graceful women almost flattened at times by costumes in gold brocade and the sort of crinoline which was called a «guardainfantas», high born gentlemen (the Duke of Pastrana next

His portrait of The Queen Mariana of Austria *is one of Carreño's finest works.*

soles held up by golden lions of the fragile widowed queen, Mariana, dressed like a nun with a wide black veil; then, of the King first as a child, then as a youth dressed in black, later, as a young man in armour adorned with bands of gay colours, always noble in his bearing and truly regal, but with a white complexion and the protruding lip of the final products of a race exhausted by consanguineous marriages. We also find traditional repertory in his work: the buffoon Bazán, the frightful fat dwarf Eugenia Vallejo, called «the Monster», and whom he first painted dressed and then nude and crowned with vine leaves like Bacchus». Carreño began painting when the decadence had begun. There is something in his painting that makes him a melancholy notary of the end of an epoch. Carreño's great quality lies in having been able to capture in paint the sickly atmosphere characteristic of the ephemeral reign of Charles II.

St. Sebastian, *a painting showing Carreño's boundless mastery of his art.*

the time; that of *Charles II*, showing the influence of Velázquez, its good composition reminding us of *Las Meninas*, soberly painted with a use of colour harmonising pleasingly with the sickly figure of the monarch; that of *Queen Mariana de Austria*, and that of *Potemkin*, the famous ambassador of Catherine of Russia to the Spanish court, with lively colouring as in Rubens, applied to the canvas with a Venetian technique. Another picture by Carreño de Miranda of special interest and in the Prado Museum is the one entitled *St. Sebastian,* which reveals the undeniable qualities of this Asturian painter.

As a court painter, Carreño could not eschew the traditional repertoire of portraits of buffoons. This series includes his painting of Eugenia Martínez Vallejo, «the Monster», *produced in 1680, when the six-year-old girl from Bárcena was brought to court that her physical singularity could be contemplated.*

to his fine horse), ecclesiastical dignitaries, foreign ambassadors, (the Russian Potemkin, with his dark red tunic and his furs). It is usual to call Carreño the Spanish Van Dyck and this is understandable; but is a Van Dyck in a minor key, more melancholy and muted».

The many paintings by Carreño de Miranda on religious subjects can be found in various museums, especially in the Louvre, and in churches: there are four canvases of his in the Madrid churches of Santiago, Hospital of La Orden Tercera and others, the best known perhaps being the frescoes at San Antonio of Los Portugueses.

Carreño is an excellent portrait painter, the best of the followers of Velázquez without any doubt. Among his portrait in the Prado, the most worthy of mention are that of *The Duke of Pastrana*, subtly reflecting the Spanish spirit of

The Relief of Genoa by the Second Marquis of Santa Cruz, *a painting by Antonio de Pereda showing the influence of the Venetian school on this painter from Valladolid.*

PEREDA

The son of a painter from Valladolid, Antonio de Pereda y Salgado was born in Valladolid in 1608 and died in 1678. Pereda painted a large quantity of pictures on religious subjects for churches in Castile, especially in Madrid, where he completed his studies as a painter. In 1635, he was chosen to collaborate on the decoration of the Salon de Reinos, but the enmity of the Count-Duke of Olivares impeded him from gaining access to the court. A supplier of religious paintings to Madrid convents, Antonio de Pereda devoted almost all his professional life to painting pictures of this kind. According to Valeriano Bozal, «Pereda specialised in a more or less moralistic type of painting similar to that of Valdés Leal, full of rhetorical elements, still life and fables. For his part, Paul Guinard states that Pereda's work is «very uneven». Experienced in practice but lacking in culture (even if one hesitated to believe the anecdote of Palomino's according to which the painter, although he was unable to read, collected unusual prints). He is incapable of renewing evangelical or monastic subjects by personal emotion; in one of his best pictures –the great *Wedding of the Virgin* painted in 1643 for his native city and now in Saint Sulpice in Paris– the charming group of young Castilians, companions of the Virgin with mottled costumes and a reserved grace, is more interesting than the main characters».

Possibly Pereda was a somewhat frustrated painter through having had to devote himself almost exclusively to the painting of religious commissions which impeded any creative flights. In spite of all this, according to Guinard, «Pereda is particularly outstanding as a master in the evocation of «silent lives», of the quality of matter, of the mysterious reflections of rare and familiar objects– precious materials jewels, flowers, fruit which he engulfs in a warm and attenuated light. A painter of still life, he is the great poet of the *Vanities*. He sings of the triumph of redemption over death, joining this subject to that of the Passion, foreshadowed in the childhood of Christ: the child Jesus, carrying the cross, appears on a field strewn with flowers, crowns and skulls».

The work of Pereda is dispersed through several foreign museums in Paris, Marseilles, Vienna, Moscow, Lisbon... and paintings of his are kept, apart from those in the churches, in the Lázaro Galdiano Museum and in the Academy of St. Fernando. In the Prado he is represented by the paintings entitled *Relief of Genoa by the Marquis of Santa Cruz*, of Venetian influence, and *St. Peter Delivered by an Angel.*

In this painting by Pereda entitled St. Peter freed by an angel *the painter's excellent gifts can be appreciated as regards religious themes; there are, at the present time, many of his religiously-inspired works still hang in churches throughout Spain.*

Goya painted his magnificent, celebrated Self-Portrait *between 1817 and 1819. In this small painting –46 x 35 cms.– the face of the painter is depicted with all the dramatic vigour impressed on it over the years.*

GOYA

Francisco de Goya y Lucientes is one of the most relevant figures of universal painting of all time, one of these exceptional people for whom the adjective genius is not sufficient. His human personality is so vigorous, his creative capacity so rich and plentiful and his work so varied and dazzling that the name of Goya as a painter resists any cataloguing in a compartment of the history of art. Goya as a subject is so controversial and exciting, but difficult and dangerous at the same time. Because Goya and his art astonish, burn, irritate, obsess, disgust, hallucinate, hypnotise and give rise in us to contradictory sentiments and changing ideas. Rafael Alberti was able to see this and express it in this memorable poem:

Sweetness, violation,
laughter, violence
smiles, blood,
gallows, fairground
There is a mad devil pursuing
light and shadows with a knife.

For you I keep an eye in the fire.
I bite off your head
I make your bones crunch. I suck out
the snail burrowing in one ear.
I bury only your legs
in the mud.
One leg
Another leg.
Strike.
Flee!
But stay to see
to die without dying...

Goya, it is true, enchants and excites, impresses, upsets, attracts, repels, subverts our reflections and submerges us in his oceanic creative magma. Looking at a picture of Soya's everything is possible except indifference.

The great painter was born in Fuendetodos, some 50 kilometres from Saragossa on 30th March 1746 and died in Bordeaux on the night of the 15th to the 16th April 1828. While his father who was a gilder was working in the capital of Aragon, the future painter of *The Naked Maja* began to study in the Escuelas Pias de Zaragoza where he had his first lessons in painting from an artist named José Luzán, a mediocre artist, and a servile follower of the strictly academic approach.

It is possible that the most important happening in the years Goya spent in Saragossa was that he got to know a group of artists whose most outstanding member was Francisco Bayeu, who went to Madrid in 1763 where he began to work under the orders of Mengs. Goya also wanted to change his scene so he went to Madrid during that year. He suffered a great disappointment when he tried to get into the Fine Arts Academy of San Fernando and failed

The painter Francisco Bayeu –*Goya's brother-in-law*–, and Josefa Bayeu –*his wife*–. Of the former, D'Ors affirms that it is «*probably the highest point reached by pictorial virtuosity*».

The Robed Maja *and* The Naked Maja *are two of Goya's most popular works and perhaps amongst the best-loved in universal art.* The Naked Maja *is an enchantingly human, sensual nude, full of feminine grace.*

to be accepted. Three years later, in 1766, he once more failed in his attempt to get in.

In 1770, Goya went to Rome, and things went better for him in Italy. The following year he won second prize in the Competition for the Parma Academy of Fine Arts. He returned to Spain and did some work in his home province.

In 1773, he returned to Madrid, where he married Josefa Bayeu; this was an important step in Goya's life, as he could now settle in the capital of Spain thanks to the help of his brother-in-law, Francisco, with whom he had worked previously. One supposes that through Bayeu, Goya succeeded in getting Mengs to commission him to do a series of cartoons for the famous tapestries of the Royal Factory of Santa Bárbara. It was the first opportunity of any importance Goya had to show his talent as a painter. With this work his economic situation improved. Valeriano Bozal writes that «The first of these cartoons reveal the decisive influence of Bayeu, from which he would soon be free. In general, we can say that the cartoons were what introduced him to the path of liberty which in religious painting –tightly bound to severe norms– would never have been allowed».

In 1780, Goya was admitted to the Royal Academy of Fine Arts of San Fernando and Jovellanos, which then had enormous influence over official circles, and offered him its protection.

The opportunity he was given to paint some frescoes in

These two paintings, of The Marquise of Villafranca *and* Queen María Luisa with «tontillo», *show Goya's original concept of portrait painting, in which he rejected any aesthetic concessions and sought to portray truth without letting his brush betray his inviolable personal ethic.*

The Duke and Duchess of Osuna and their children, *another of Goya's masterly works in the Prado Museum.*

the church of El Pilar in Saragossa was to serve him to show for the first time in an explicit and decisive way that he had broken with the academic rules which tried to keep painting in a state of orthodoxy and curb artistic creativity. His brother-in-law, Bayeu, reproached him when he saw the frescoes for what he considered frivolous execution when really it was nothing more than a sample of the free creative demonstration of Goya's genius.

But Bayeu was the official director of the work on the church, and Goya had to modify his drawings, which he did much against his will; however, Goya was Goya, and was not disposed to give in. Thus he came to a serious decision, very much characteristic of his impetuous temperament: he broke with Bayeu. After that he went his own way in art, no longer submitting to the dictates of others, but to his own powerful genius. In order to solve economic problems, Goya had to accept several commissions and in 1783 he painted the *Portrait of The Count of Florida-blanca*, and, the year after, *The Preaching of St. Bernardino of Sienna*.

He was appointed painter to the King in 1786, which brought him an annual pension of 15,000 «reales de vellón». Now that his economic situation was easier he could devote himself to his own artistic projects and painted several pictures, among them the one entitled, *The San*

In this portrait of Charles IV, *brilliantly coloured, Goya brings out once more his extraordinary skill as a portraitist.*

The Portrait of Queen María Luisa, *another revealing masterpiece by Goya.*

Isidro Plain. A serene lucidity is evident in the work of Goya between 1786 and 1792. His canvases are the result of the self-confidence he had acquired. For about six years, everything seems to go well for him artistically, socially and as regards health. In 1789, Charles IV appointed him court painter and this is the time of his most joyful cartoons: *Blind Man's Buff, and The Village Wedding.*

But suddenly, in 1792, misfortune came his way and tortured his spirit. His work also suffered a change of considerable proportions. His world became different and gained a dimension between lucidity and visceral, reflecting the complex human condition.

In autumn 1792, Goya went on a journey to Cadiz and during this he fell ill and was never to be really cured. He was ill for many months and when he was partly recovered remained deaf for the rest of his life.

After his illness, Goya's work grew and acquired a profound and inimitable style, showing us on the one hand witches sabbaths and on the other terrifyingly lucid views of human life. The painter himself alluded to the change in his artistic talent in a letter he wrote on 4th January 1794 to his friend the writer and diplomat Don Bernardo de Iriarte: «To occupy my mortifying imagination on the subject of my illness, I decided to paint a series of pictures in which I have succeeded in making observations which commissioned

A charming portrait of Queen María Luisa on horseback, *a painting bearing the unmistakable hallmark of Goya.*

In this portrait of Charles IV, *Goya once more produces a masterpiece within the canons of his own personal aesthetic.*

work does not really allow and in which caprice and invention are now let free».

About this time, it appears that Goya painted *The Mad House, The Burial of the Sardine, Bullfight* and *The Procession of the Flagellants,* among other works in which it is not difficult to see the profound change in Goya's aesthetic style. About 1795 he painted the Duchess of Alba and her husband. It would appear that between 1795 and 1797 the relationship between the painter and the Duchess, although it is impossible to know the degree of intimacy they enjoyed, became close, and it would not be hazardous to say there was at least the appearance of an erotic element in their association.

In 1798, Goya painted the magnificent frescoes of San Antonio de la Florida and about 1799 did a series of etchings called *The Caprices*. Goya was now quite mature as an artist and could dominate at will all types of technique and was capable of all types of expression; he had become the critical, esoteric Goya but also profoundly, almost cruelly human, he had broken with the past and with his fierce

creativeness frenziedly rubbed out the least vestige of conformism.

In the first year of the XIX century, Goya finished one of his great masterpieces: *The family of Charles IV*. This is a really prodigious example of execution and an astonishingly implacable psychological study of those painted.

But Goya had still to live through the drama of the Peninsular War and to paint works such as *Madrid, the 2nd of May 1808: the fight with the Mamelukes, and Madrid, the 3rd of May 1808: the shootings on Prince Pius Mountain*, two of his most impressive and justly famous paintings. At the same time he painted (between 1812 and 1814) *Two Drinkers, The Water Seller* and *The Colossus*.

In 1815, he painted his well-known *Self-portrait*, and four years later produced the famous series of the so called «black paintings». In 1823 when the «hundred thousand sons of Saint Louis» invaded Spain, Goya had to go into hiding and the following year he went first to Paris and then to Bordeaux. He fell ill in 1825, went to Madrid in 1826 and on returning to Bordeaux continued to paint. One of his last paintings is *The Milk Maid from Bordeaux*, and he died without being able to finish the portrait of *José Pio de Molina* which he had started in 1828.

Goya is an artist who liberated forms and ideas. He painted as he wanted and what he wanted. For him, after reaching the summit of his creative powers there were no barriers to impede his radical sincerity and to stand in his way, in the way of truth with no concessions given. When we look at the diversity of his popular spectacle it is sometimes vulgar and maybe coarse, but always spontaneous and dynamic and Goya smiles with irony mixed with comprehending pity. But when he come face to face with the vanity and the corruption of the court he is implacable in pointing out in his pictures the viciousness he sees around him and does not hesitate to paint Charles IV, María Luisa, Godoy or Ferdinand VII as he really sees them, which in this case is like giving a personal opinion of them as distinguished persons. Goya uses his art to make a pitiful, moving cry against the horrors of war. Finally, self-absorbed and taking into the very core of his being a vision of the world plagued by stigmas of all kinds, Goya, filled with pain, revulsion and ire, twists the forms of his aesthetic and creates the so-called «black paintings» which, revoltingly fascinating, herald much of later painting, including the finest aspects of expressionism.

It is easy to perceive a similar critical spirit in the art as Goya as we find in the literary works of Quevedo and Valle-Inclán. The Quevedo of *Los Sueños and El Buscón* is as near to Goya after 1792 as Valle-Inclán is to both in *El Ruedo Ibérico*.

The magic of his use of colour and perfect technical execution are reflected in Goya's portrait of Ferdinand VII with royal mantle.

Goya's portraits–like this one of Ferdinand VII at an encampment– *are a valuable source of historic information.*

«Valle-Inclán –writes Ferrater Mora– appears to rejoice in his neat pictures (but this will be seen as one of his recourses) in stereotyped gestures, in well-described figures that do not move but only keep all their potential for moving in their immobility. It is not even necessary to describe a complete figure: it is enough to show a hand outstretched, and expression on the face, the pleat of a dress. It is not necessary to describe a thing, it is sufficient to point out a facet». Is that not what Goya is essentially doing in his «black paintings»? Goya is a highly gifted artist. He can attack any subject, no technical obstacle lies in his path. «He has painted –says Ortega y Gasset– all subjects divine, human, diabolical, and fantasmagorical. He has left out none of these themes, from the religious picture, allegory, and perspective (San Antonio de la Florida) to anecdotic engravings and caricature. I have asked myself more than once whether it is not this universality of Goya's work which is a possible cause of the fact that it has been difficult to try even to define his organic unity».

This is true. Everyone tries to penetrate into the world of Goya, but no one can come out with anything better than a partial analysis of his work. It seems as though the magnitude and the abysmal profundity of his art had put fear into the minds of potential students of his work. Goya is the best represented painter in the Prado with 114 paintings and 50 drawings on show. This is a treasure of incalculable value. *The Family of Charles IV,* one of Goya's most famous pictures, is considered by many cognoscenti to be the best painting he ever did. Of course, it is one

Goya's inexhaustible creative force allowed him to make original discoveries with regard to colouring, as in this Portrait of the Marquis of Villafranca and Duke of Alba.

Goya's artistic vigour is fully reflected in this splendid portrait, perfect in its execution, of General Urrutia.

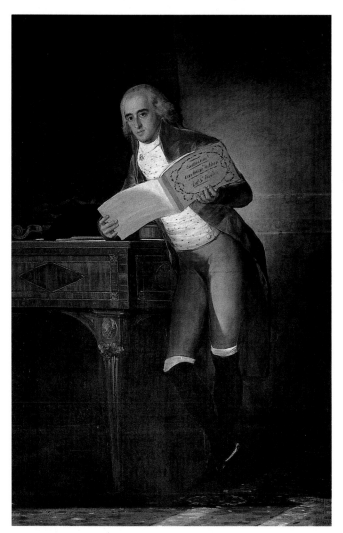

The San Isidro fields –*painted in around 1788– is a study for a cartoon to be used for a tapestry. In it, Goya, with his powerful narrative skill, shows us one of the traditions of Madrid. In the foreground is a typical XVIII scene. The centre of the picture is occupied by happy people on a religious procession, or* romería, *and in the background, diffused, is the skyline of the Madrid of those days.*

The Milkmaid from Bordeaux *is one of Goya's last works and was painted after a journey to Madrid in 1826, when the artist was 80 years old.*

The work, entitled The Travelling Players, *is a fine example of the feeling for colour so characteristic of Goya's painting.*

Boys playing at soldiers, Boys picking fruit *and* Boys blowing up a bladder *are paintings on cardboard. Apparently due to the mediation of Bayeu, Goya succeeded in getting a commission from Mengs for a series of cartoons for the famous tapestries made at the royal factory of Santa Bárbara. This was Goya's first chance to show his mettle as an artist. The experience of painting cartoons was for Goya one of the most fruitful and interesting of his early years as a painter in Madrid.*

These three charming paintings on cardboard –The Little Giants, Boys climbing a tree *and* Boys with a Mastiff– *also designs for reproduction in tapestry form, are further examples of Goya's vigorous popular vein, always present in his work. «Generally speaking –writes Valeriano Bozal–, we can say that the cartoons were what trained Goya as a painter and at the same time what introduced him to the paths of freedom of form which, in religious painting, so tightly bound to strict norms, he would never have been able to follow».*

Two fine cartoons, The Washerwomen *and* The Flower-sellers *or* Spring, *in which Goya depicts scenes from popular life. On Goya's cartoons for tapestries, Margherite Abbruzzese says that the artist «hits just the right note, with growing maturity of expression and a mastery of media after 1776-1777».*

Girls with jugs, *a cartoon typical of Goya's style, and* The Nincompoop, *with its subtle grace. In the face of the «nincompoop», tossed on a blanket to the amusement of four women, can be seen the human sadness of the professional clown, never completely hidden by circus make-up.*

The Quarrel at the New Inn, *a curious painting on a popular theme bearing the hallmark of Goya.*

The Snowfall, or Winter *shows Goya's great power to capture reality.*

The Threshing Floor, or Summer, The Drunkard *and* The Blind Man with his Guitar *are works of powerful realism in which Goya gives free rein to his creative powers and passion for colour. Underlying the social customs depicted in the cartoons is always an aura of refreshing vitality.*

The Game of Bat and Ball, *a splendid cartoon in which Goya once more demonstrates his unsurpassed pictorial gifts. Goya's cartoons lay forgotten until they were transferred to the Prado Museum, where they are now on exhibition.*

The Crockery Seller, The Swing and The Dance on the banks of the Manzanares are clear examples of Goya's expressive language in paint. The first is a large cartoon –259 x 220 cms.– and was painted in 1779 as the model for a tapestry for the Princes' Bedroom in El Pardo Palace. After consolidating his artistic mastery painting cartoons for tapestries, Goya never looked back. His artistic career went triumphantly forward until he had formulated his own aesthetic, which was to revolutionise all painting in the XIX century and would leave an indelible mark on world art, influencing the work of grate painters to come.

In The Hermitage of San Isidro on a feast day, *Goya achieves singularly original effects. The figures in the foreground stand out as dynamic forms, with a lively sense of playfulness, whilst the figures in the background form a human mass of vigorous force at the foot of the church.*

Blind Man's Buff *is a prodigy of cosmopolitan grace and colourist joy. The figures really appear to be moving to the rhythm of their own evident enjoyment. Goya achieves an admirable portrayal of a charming scene, and the work is full of life and aesthetic good taste.*

The popular vein always latent in Goya takes on evident protagonism in this painting of The Wedding. *The infant figure lifting its arms on one side of the picture is typical of Goya, and all the figures are studied and described with that love of the popular which springs from Goya's brush irrepressibly. His makes rich use of colour, too, applying it with admirable precision.*

The Grape Harvest, or autumn, *is one of the most beautiful of the cartoons Goya painted for the Royal Tapestry Factory. Goya's first cartoons are, according to Paul Guinard «on the same level as those by Ramón Bayeu and José del Castillo, but show, and this is their principal point of interest, how Goya broadened and humanised the initial formula».*

The Tobacco Watch, Hunting Party *and* The Stilts *belong to the series of cartoons called «the jobs and the days». Goya treats these cartoons, particularly* The Stilts, *in a more concentrated way. «It is –points out Paul Guinard– the moment when Goya renews the formula for his cartoons, which appear to exceed themselves, replacing them with minor formulas, treating popular themes as living, palpitating sketches». This is exactly what we see in the three paintings reproduced on this page.*

of his masterpieces; it is enormous, being 280 by 336 cms., and in it Goya shows off all his portentous artistic faculties. But what is pleasant and not only produces surprise in the person who looks at the picture, but a certain sort of sympathy with the artist, more than the masterly composition and the firm brushstroke, is the halo of irony which seems to emanate from the whole atmosphere of the painting. Goya has certainly made no concessions in painting the portrait of these people. He has not borne in mind their station and paints them as they are: with their element of vulgarity and lust implacably reflected on the nasty features of their self-satisfied faces. The colour, superbly impasted, produces a singular effect: its gaudiness accentuates the crude reality, putting into greater relief the human aspect of the people and the atmosphere of the court.

Masterpieces too are *The Naked Maja*, an enchantingly human picture, in which the body of the woman is of an appealing grace. The composition is masterly, the execution and colour truly astounding. *Madrid, 2nd of May 1808: the fight with the Mamelukes* is an oil painting of huge dimensions –266 by 345 cms.– in which Goya has been able to assemble several dramatic effects which give the onlooker the strange feeling that he is really present at the rebellious beginning of a popular uprising against the French; the colour is full of life and a vigorous dynamism in its depicting of the bloody spectacle; *Madrid, 3rd of May 1808: the shootings on the Principe Pío Mountain*, also an enormous canvas and possibly artistically superior to the former, in which the dramatic vibration is more intense in its reflection of the scene of the executions in all their terrible grandeur, in all their cruelty and also in all their sinister political expediency –it can be said that in this painting Goya is at his most characteristic–; then his splendid *Self-portrait,* painted between 1817 and 1819, in which the painter appears before us in all the dramatic vigour which the years have imprinted on his features. Perfect in execution, it is a *self-portrait* in which Goya succeeds in accentuating the expression by counterpoising the light illuminating the face with the shadows of the background.

The Sunshade *is one of the cartoons painted by Goya for the Royal Tapestry Factory in which the colour range is amongst the most varied and splendid.*

These three cartoons by Goya, The Kite, The Picnic and The Maja and the Cloaked Men *belong to the group painted between 1776 and 1780, that is to say, during the first period the artist devoted to creating models for the Royal Tapestry Factory. In them, his colouring is bright and shining, announcing the unsurpassed Goya of works to come. In these cartoons, Goya, we must insist, initiated the dazzling revolution in colour which has not been surpassed even today, and which connects him directly with the great masters of XIX and XX century painting, including, needless to say, Pablo Ruiz Picasso himself.*

Goya painted this magnificent canvas, Madrid, 2 May 1808: the Fight with the Mamelukes, *in 1814, commissioned, it would seem, by Ferdinand VII, to perpetuate «our glorious uprising against the tyrant of Europe». This is one of those rare paintings which can certainly be described as the work of a genius. Goya excels himself, capturing the dramatic atmosphere of those crucial days in the Spanish capital with truly prodigious realism.*

Madrid, 3 May 1808: the shootings on the Príncipe Pío Mountain *is an impressive oil in which Goya condemns the cruel events of the time from the depths of his rebellious soul. The French soldiers, whose faces remain unseen, their gesture and attitude sufficient, aim their rifles at a group of patriots they have before them. One of these, in the centre, stands out. He is wearing a white shirt and lifts his arms in a manly gesture. This is one of Goya's most remarkable masterpieces.*

Goya, as can be seen in this portrait of The Infanta Doña María Josefa, *never falsified nature in order to favour his subject.*

The characteristic brightness of the Goya's use of colour is clear in this portrait of Don Luis of Bourbon, Prince of Parma.

An evocative portrait of The Infante Don Carlos María Isidro, *brother of Ferdinand VII.*

Goya was always averse to flattering with the paint brush. Here, his portrait of The Infante Don Antonio Pascual.

Witches' Sabbath (Asmodea). *This and such other works as* The Execution *and* Una manola: Doña Leocadia Zorrilla, *on the next page, belong to the surprising aesthetic of the Goya of Los Caprichos. «Gracefulness and anguish appear, as Paul Guinard so rightly says, intimately intermingled in Los Caprichos. It was through reproductions from this collection that XIX-century Europeans discovered Goya. In France he become a source of inspiration, early and continually renewed, for the greatest artists»... Delacroix and Manet, amongst others, tried to follow in Goya's footsteps.*

Fight with Cudgels, *one of the «dark paintings», with its obsessive and gloomy atmosphere.*

The Colossus, *an allegorical painting symbolising war, and* Saturn devouring one of his children, *a work in which Goya appears to seek to portray the anguish of a man losing his vital energies.*

Una Manola: Doña Leocadia Zorrilla *and* The Execution.

These four works –Witches' Sabbath, The Reading, Two Friars *and* Two Women with a Man– *belong to the enigmatic series of works known as the «dark paintings», which Goya produced to decorate his country house, the well-known «Quinta del Sordo» (Deaf Man's Estate) between 1814 and 1822.*

The Three Fates (Atropos) *is one of Goya's famous «dark paintings», characterised by a strange deforming aesthetic. Goya appears to have begun this series after half-recovering from illness, which would explain the pessimistic vein.*

Both the Procession to the Hermitage of San Isidro *and the* Pilgrimage to the San Isidro fountain *appear to be seen through the deforming lens of a Quevedo or a Valle Inclán. Goya transforms this popular theme into a real witches' sabbath. All his so-called «dark paintings» follow the same twisted aesthetic canon.*

This portrait of Feliciana Bayeu, the artist's daughter, from around 1788, shows Francisco Bayeu's mastery of the portrait.

FRANCISCO BAYEU

Born in Saragossa in 1734, died in Madrid in 1795, Francisco Bayeu belonged to a family of painters. His brother Ramón, born in 1746, also did some thirty cartoons with popular types and scenes for the Royal Tapestry Factory. Another brother, Manuel, the youngest of the three, and also a painter who became a Carthusian monk, painted numerous pictures on religious subjects.

Apart from a large quantity of cartoons for tapestries, Francisco Bayeu painted a considerable number of religious pictures, the majority of which are still kept in churches in Aragon. He was much influenced by Mengs, who protected him and worked with him on the decoration of the Royal Palace about 1763. The author of the ceiling paintings *The Fall of the Giants* and *The Surrender of Granada*, Bayeu was appointed court painter in 1767 and Director of the Academy in 1788. The brother-in-law of Goya, Bayeu did not have anything like the creative strength of his famous relative. He was an excellent portrait painter and some of his likenesses are, in the opinion of Paul Guinard, «perfectly worthy of his brother-in-law Goya, to the extent that the authorship of some portraits in still under discussion, such as, for example, that of the man in a large hat in the Saragossa Museum».

Francisco Bayeu is represented in the Prado by the canvas entitled *Paseo de las Delicias in Madrid*, a small graceful sketch in rococo style and of indisputable artistic quality.

Olympus: Battle of the Giants and El Paseo de las Delicias in Madrid, *two characteristic works by Francisco Bayeu. The first was painted in 1764 as a sketch for the ceiling of the Palace in Madrid; the second, completed in around 1785, is a sketch for the cartoon for a tapestry in El Pardo Palace.*

The Adoration of the Magi, *one of the works by Fray Juan Bautista Mayno exhibited in the Prado Museum.*

MAYNO, RIZI...

Among the Spanish painters represented in the Prado Museum who can be catalogued as in the second rank compared with those already mentioned, the most noteworthy are Mayno and Rizi.

Juan Bautista Mayno was considered to be from Milan until his certificate of baptism was discovered and it was seen that he was born in Pastrana (Guadalajara) in 1568. Mayno was formed artistically in Toledo and the influence of El Greco can be seen in his work. He became a member of the Dominican Order and painted religious pictures in Seville and Madrid. He was art teacher to Philip III and president of the jury which declared Velázquez the winner of a competition which took place in 1627 on the subject of the expulsion of the Moors, and he collaborated in the decoration of the Salon de Reinos in the Retiro. Mayno died in 1649.

Francisco Rizi was born in 1608 and was a painter of the Toledo Cathedral in 1653 and of the Court in 1656, besides being the author of some large altar paintings. Rizi painted the decorations in the theatre of the Retiro and together with Carreño did some frescoes for the Church of San Antonio of Los Portugueses and Toledo Cathedral. He died in 1685 and is represented in the Prado with the work entitled *Auto de Fe in the Plaza Mayor in Madrid.*

Francisco Rizi was the younger brother of Fray Juan Rizi (1600-1681), a Benedictine scholar, theologian, mathematician and geometrician who was in charge of several monasteries. He painted a good number of pictures and wrote a book entitled *On learned painting*, illustrated with drawings done by himself.

Other painters with works on show in the Prado are:

Pedro Orrente, born in Montalegre about 1570 and died in 1645, a pupil of El Greco who produced several Biblical pictures, including *The adoration of the Shepherds* in the Prado, and some religious works in the cathedrals of Toledo and Valencia.

Valdés Leal (1622-1690) a painter of eschatological themes whose main work, of uneven merit, is in Seville, with has several works in the Prado, including *Jesus debating with the Doctors.*

José Leonardo, born in Calatayud in 1605 who died in the same town in 1656, among whose paintings on show in the Prado *The Surrender of Juliers* is outstanding.

Juan de Arellano (1614-1676) with his canvas *The flower bowl.*

Francisco de Herrera, the Elder, born in Seville towards the end of the XVI century and died about 1657, a teacher of Velázquez with works in the Louvre and the Prado Museum *(The Triumph of St. Hermenegildo).*

José Antolínez, born in Madrid in 1635 who died in the same town in 1675. He has several religious works in the Prado *(The death of Mary Magdalene)* and in the Lázaro Galdiano Gallery and some other works on profane subjects in Munich and Copenhagen.

Luis Paret y Alcázar, born in Madrid of a French father in 1741 and died in 1799, with works in the Prado *(Fernando VII as Prince of Asturias,* and *Charles III eating before his court),* in the Lázaro Galdiano Gallery, and in the Academy of San Fernando; Pedro Machuca, Juan de Flandes, Caxés and others.

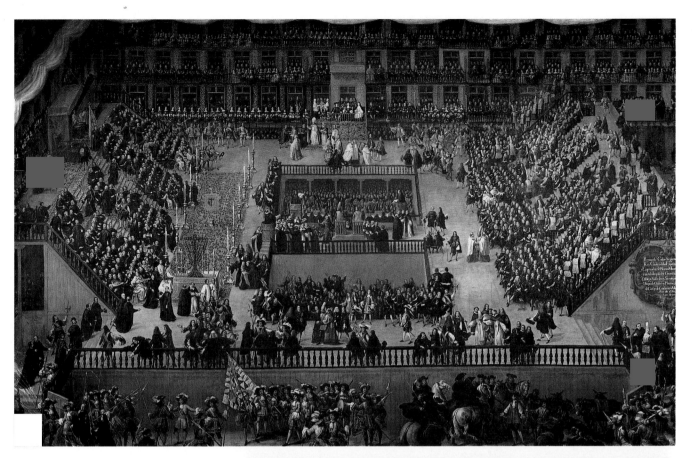

Auto de Fe in the Plaza Mayor in Madrid, *by Francisco Rizi.*

San Benito's Supper, *a painting by Fray Juan Andrés Rizi, demonstrating a delicate use of colour harmonising with the spirit of the theme. A profoundly religious atmosphere pervades this painting, which emanates a transcendental air highlighting even more strongly the still life painted on the table.*

Pedro de Orrente –born in the late-XVI century and died in the mid-XVII– is represented in the Prado Museum with a collection of paintings on Biblical themes, amongst which the most outstanding is The Adoration of the Shepherds, *a beautifully executed work with harmonious shades of colour and fine composition which bear witness to the excellence of this artist.*

Jesus debating with the Doctors, *by Valdés Leal, a Sevillian painter who specialised in religious themes. A friend and contemporary of Murillo who died a paralytic in 1690. Most of his work is conserved in his native city.*

The Surrender of Juliers, *by José Leonardo, shows the artist's considerable talent for depicting historical themes. Leonardo was born in Calatayud in 1605 and died in the same city in 1656. He produced rather few works as illness forced him to give up painting in 1648. The* Surrender of Juliers *is a painting featuring outstanding use of colour and rather exaggerated composition. Its artistic merit resides fundamentally in the skilfully wrought contrast between the group of figures in the foreground and the austere schematic landscape which serves as the backcloth.*

Flower piece, *by Juan de Arellano (1614-1676), a painter who specialised in floral themes. Arellano took an architectural approach to the arrangement of his flowers and possessed an innate good taste when it came to applying colour. His flower paintings are as evocative as they are attractive.*

The Death of Mary Magdalene, *by the Madrilenian painter José Antolínez (1635-1675). A specialist in religious themes, Antolínez left a large body of works.*

The Triumph
of Saint
Hermenegildo,
*an allegorical
painting by
Francisco
de Herrera
(1627-1685).*

Charles III eating before his court, *and* The Oath of Ferdinand VII as Prince of Asturias, *by Luis Paret y Alcázar. Paret's paintings show him to be one of the Spanish artists who best assimilated the aesthetics of the French Louis XV style. He was also an observant chronicler life in Madrid under Charles III.*

The Royal Couples *shows the riding festival which took place in Aranjuez in spring 1770. The author of this work, Luis Paret y Alcázar, won distinction as a painter of this type of scene. Paret, born in Madrid of a French father and a Madrilenian mother, was something of a globetrotter. He lived in Rome, Paris and Puerto Rico, where he was deported by Charles III.*

In his Descent from the Cross, *Pedro Machuca reveals his profound knowledge of architecture. This is a perfectly drawn work, though the subject certainly does not lend itself to an architectural framework. Not for nothing, though, was Machuca the master builder of the Palace of Charles I in Granada.*

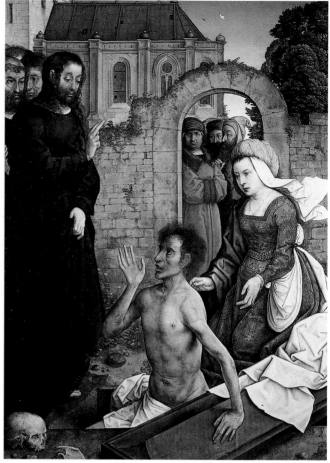

In its structure and, particularly, the woman depicted behind the body of Lazarus, this painting by Juan de Flandes, The Resurrection of Lazarus, *reveals the Flemish origins of the artist, a protégé of Isabel the Catholic.*

The Fable of Leda, a copy of Correggio's original by Eugenio Caxés or Cajés (1574-1634). For this copy and another, entitled The Rape of Ganymedes, *whose original is also by Correggio, Caxés was paid 1,500 reales in 1604.*

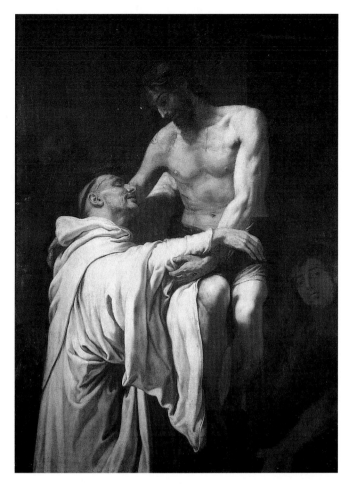

Christ Embracing Saint Bernard, *a work by the Valencian artist Ribalta, whose work, which combines religious drama and gloomy naturalism, is clearly influenced by Correggio and Caravaggio. Nevertheless, Ribalta's style, full of vigour, remains within the aesthetic –and temperamental– canons of great Spanish religious painting.*

Portrait of Bartolomé Esteban Murillo, *by Miguel de Tobar (1678-1758), one of the most faithful followers of Murillo's aesthetic.*

In this portrait of Don Francisco Fernández de Córdoba y Mendoza, *by Fernando del Rincón de Figueroa, the most striking feature is the vigour with which the subject's face is painted.*

Villandrando shows his qualities as a portrait painter in this full-length portrait of Philip IV and the dwarf «Soplillo». This is a well-finished, academic work of undeniable artistic quality.

Magnificent Self-Portrait by Sebastián Muñoz (1637-1690), of austere colour and perfect execution.

852.

Portrait of Queen Doña Margarita of Austria, *by Bartolomé González, a painter born 1564 and died 1627. He was, along with Villandrando, one of the most highly esteemed portrait artists in the court of Philip III. This work, exhibited in the Prado Museum, shows González's minute attention to detail, particularly as regards the clothing.*

123

This painting –very much obeying the baroque canon–, entitled The Burial of the Lord of Orgaz *–and reminiscent of El Greco's famous painting–, is one of several works by Miguel Jacinto Mélendez (1679-1734) in the Prado Museum.*

La Prudent Abigail, *by Juan Antonio de Frías y Escalante, a painter born in Córdoba in 1633 and died in Madrid in 1669. Despite his short life, Frías left works of considerable worth, including this painting, entitled* The Communion of St. Rose of Viterbo, *also conserved in the Prado Museum.*

The Recapture of the Island of San Cristóbal, *a painting on a historic theme by Félix Castello (1595-1651).*

The Ascent of the Montgolfier Balloon in Madrid, *by Antonio Carnicero (1748-1814).*
The Hunt of the Tabladillo *in Aranjuez, by Juan Bautista del Mazo, Velázquez's son-in-law, with whom he collaborated in several works, including* The Royal Hunt of the Wild Boar in the Woods of El Pardo.

CONTENTS

ESCUDO DE ORO, S.A. COLLECTIONS

The printing of this book was completed
in the workshops of
FISA - Escudo de Oro, S.A.
Palaudàries, 26 - Barcelona (Spain)

 Protegemos el bosque; papel procedente de cultivos forestales controlados
Wir schützen den Wald. Papier aus kontrollierten Forsten.
We protect our forests. The paper used comes from controlled forestry plantations
Nous sauvegardons la forêt: papier provenant de cultures forestières controlées